N E W   C R A F T S

PAPIER MACHE

NEW CRAFTS
PAPIER MACHE

MARION ELLIOT

PHOTOGRAPHY BY PETER WILLIAMS

LORENZ BOOKS

THIS EDITION FIRST PUBLISHED IN 1998 BY
LORENZ BOOKS

© ANNESS PUBLISHING LIMITED 1998

LORENZ BOOKS IS AN IMPRINT OF
ANNESS PUBLISHING LIMITED, HERMES HOUSE
88–89 BLACKFRIARS ROAD, LONDON SE1 8HA

THIS EDITION IS PUBLISHED IN THE USA BY
LORENZ BOOKS, ANNESS PUBLISHING INC.,
27 WEST 20TH STREET, NEW YORK, NY 10011,
(800) 354–9657

THIS EDITION DISTRIBUTED IN CANADA BY
RAINCOAST BOOKS, 8680 CAMBIE STREET,
VANCOUVER, BRITISH COLUMBIA V6P 6M9

ISBN 1 85967 619 7

A CIP CATALOGUE RECORD FOR THIS BOOK IS
AVAILABLE FROM THE BRITISH LIBRARY

PUBLISHER: JOANNA LORENZ
SENIOR EDITOR: CATHERINE BARRY
DESIGNER: LILIAN LINDBLOM
PHOTOGRAPHER: PETER WILLIAMS
STYLIST: GEORGINA RHODES
ILLUSTRATORS: LUCINDA GANDERTON AND
VANA HAGGERTY

PRINTED IN HONG KONG

10 9 8 7 6 5 4 3 2 1

DISCLAIMER
The author and publishers have made every effort to ensure that all the instructions in this book are accurate and safe, and therefore cannot accept liability
for any resulting injury, damage or loss to persons or property however it may arise.

CONTENTS

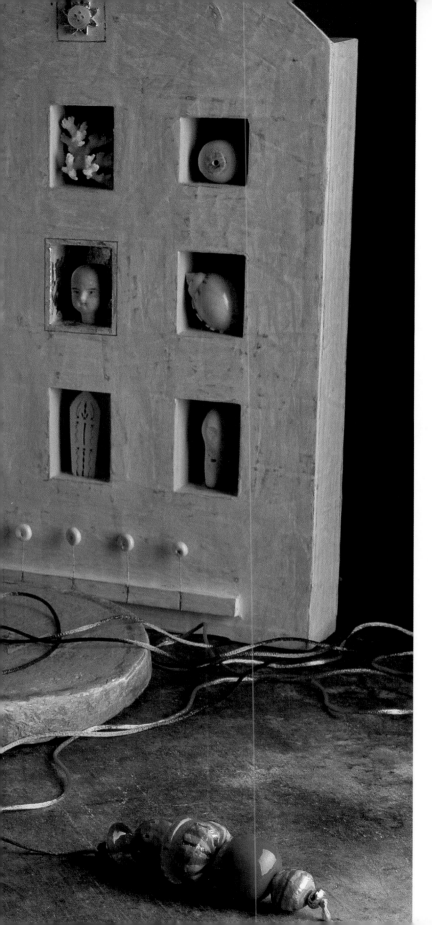

INTRODUCTION

PAPIER MACHE IS A CHAMELEON CRAFT, CAPABLE OF IMITATING MANY DIFFERENT MATERIALS. ITS VERSATILITY AND, OF COURSE, LOW COST, HAS MADE IT ONE OF THE MOST POPULAR METHODS OF MAKING BOTH BEAUTIFUL AND USEFUL OBJECTS FOR MANY CENTURIES. ONCE USED TO MAKE ARTICLES AS DIVERSE AS A HORSE-DRAWN CARRIAGE AND ARCHITECTURAL PANELS, OR MINIATURE DECORATIVE SNUFF BOXES, PAPIER MACHE CAN BE USED TO ENHANCE MODERN INTERIORS IN SIMILARLY INNOVATIVE WAYS. FUN AND EASY TO TACKLE, THE PROJECTS IN THIS BOOK HAVE BEEN DESIGNED TO INSPIRE EVEN THE NOVICE CRAFTSPERSON TO ATTEMPT THIS REWARDING CRAFT.

Left: A surprising variety and quality of objects can be made from papier mâché. Its strength and versatility have made it an ideal technique for household objects.

HISTORY OF PAPIER MACHE

PAPIER MACHE HAS AN EXCITING AND ANCIENT HISTORY, ORIGINATING IN CHINA IN THE EARLY YEARS OF THE 2ND CENTURY AD. IT HAS BEEN USED SINCE TO MAKE CHAIRS FOR ROYALTY, PANELS FOR COACHES, JEWELLERY, AND EVEN CHINESE SPEARS AND ARMOUR – THE EARLIEST KNOWN EXAMPLES. THROUGHOUT HISTORY IT HAS MADE VARIOUS APPEARANCES AS THE LATEST CRAZE, YET THE BASIC TECHNIQUES REMAIN THE SAME AS IN THE 2ND CENTURY.

Paper was first made by Ts'ai Lun, an official at the Chinese court of the Emperor Ho Ti, who developed an ingenious way of breaking down plants and rags into single fibres. The fibres were pounded to a pulp and collected on a fabric-covered frame, where they matted and dried as paper. The knowledge of paper-making spread to Japan, the Middle East and India, finally reaching Europe via Spain in the 10th century AD. The modern-day practice of recycling waste paper into moulded objects became well established in Persia and India, where craftsmen made extravagantly lacquered and embellished papier mâché pen holders from around the 15th century. Kashmir in Northern India was an important centre of this art; its products were exported to Europe during the 16th and 17th centuries as trade routes developed, and were much admired for the quality of their lacquering and their exquisitely painted decoration.

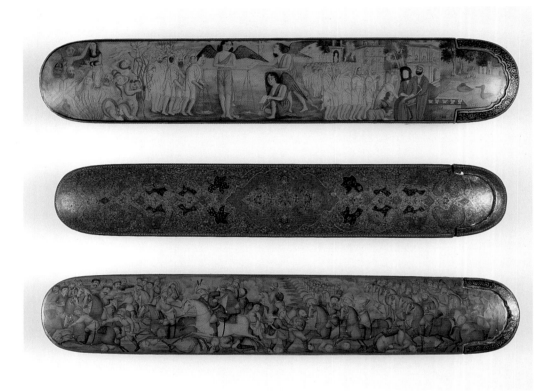

A flourishing trade in eastern goods developed, as a mania for chinoiserie – objects with Oriental motifs executed in a Western style – gripped Europe. Demand far exceeded supply, and workshops were set up, notably in France and England, to produce home-grown imitations of items such as porcelain and lacquerware. French

Above: Three lacquered papier mâché qalamdans (pen cases) from Qajar, Persia painted with religious and military scenes, 1860.

Left and right: Backs of playing cards made from papier mâché from Kashmir, India c. 1600.

panels, made from pasted paper sheets rather than pulped paper. The panels were sealed with linseed oil and dried slowly under a low heat, which made them extremely strong. They were used for everyday articles, such as furniture, and the material was ideally suited to japanning (varnishing) and painting. Clay's panels were so strong and resilient that they were also used to make the walls of horse-drawn coaches. Clay patented his invention in 1772, and by the time the

Left: Painted and lacquered papier mâché chest with ivory fringe, c. 1660.

Below: Two French papier mâché fans inlaid with mother-of-pearl and hand-painted with flowers, c. 1780.

craftsmen were intrigued by Oriental papier mâché and experimented with the medium, adding materials such as sand, glue and chalk to the pulped paper. They developed their techniques until capable of producing convincing moulded architectural ornaments in imitation of costly stucco and plasterwork. This practice was also adopted in England, where several papier mâché workshops were established, primarily in London and the Midlands.

The development of a lacquering process that compared favourably with Japanese and Chinese lacquerware also helped to establish papier mâché in Europe. Known as japanning, this quicker, less expensive technique was used widely from the 1740s in the decoration of papier mâché items such as small tables, snuff boxes and hand mirrors. In the mid-18th century Henry Clay, assistant to John Baskerville, a manufacturer from Birmingham, England, took a step forward in papier mâché production, which laid the foundations of a whole industry. Clay's innovation was to produce laminated

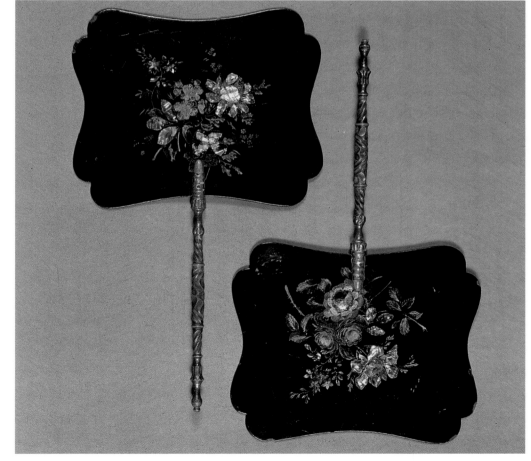

Above: Papier mâché chair with split cane seat, embellished with mother-of-pearl, c. 1840–50.

Right: Circus figures made of wood and papier mâché by Schoenhut & Co, Germany, c 1900.

patents expired in 1802, he was very wealthy. His Birmingham factory was taken over in 1816 by what was to become the most famous partnership in the papier mâché industry, Jennens and Bettridge.

Jennens and Bettridge raised papier mâché design to new heights, introducing all kinds of decorative and practical refinements. They developed a distinctive range of japanned goods inlaid with slivers of mother-of-pearl; later they included tortoiseshell, ivory and precious stones. They also patented a method of steam-moulding and pressing papier mâché panels into large-scale architectural features, such as internal walls for steamships. By 1850, Jennens and Bettridge were England's foremost

exponents of papier mâché. They had a huge workforce, with ex-employees leaving to set up their own factories. At London's Great Exhibition of 1851 in the Crystal Palace, papier mâché was hailed as an important material with a bright future, and Jennens and Bettridge exhibited a wide range of artefacts, including a child's cot, a chair and a piano. This was the heyday of papier mâché production in Europe. Manufacturing methods had become extremely sophisticated, and the resulting objects were indistinguishable from the finest lacquered wood. A huge range of items, from buttons to headboards, was produced; George Jackson and Son made stunningly ornate imitation plaster- and stuccowork ceilings and walls, and Charles Bielefield produced a papier mâché "village" of eleven houses for export to Australia.

Papier mâché was also popular in North America, and Jennens and Bettridge, and other manufacturers, were exporting their wares there before the middle of the 19th century. In 1850, when the United States' first papier mâché factory was established at Litchfield, Connecticut, English workers were brought over to teach their skills. The Litchfield Manufacturing Company was started by English-born Quaker William Allgood, and was successful from the start. The factory initially produced small ornamental items, such as fans and card cases, but then concentrated on making papier mâché versions of the area's main product, decorative clock cases. These were warmly received, and commended at the World Fair in New York in 1854. Litchfield Manufacturing merged with a clock company in 1855, but a nearby

factory, Wadhams Manufacturing Co., continued to produce papier mâché goods, such as desks and gameboards, until the outbreak of the American Civil War.

Although the Western papier mâché industries had run out of steam by the end of the 19th century, cultures who had been consistently using papier mâché continued making boxes, cases, lamp-stands, trays and frames, decorated with extremely intricate traditional designs, such as interlocking flowers, animals and scenes from court life. The tourist economies of Kashmir and Rajasthan benefit to this day.

In Mexico, remarkable papier mâché sculptures and artefacts are made throughout the year to commemorate religious festivals. The best known of these is on All Souls' Day, known as the Day of the Dead, when Mexicans build ornate shrines and prepare meals for departed relatives whom they believe will come to visit. Brightly coloured skeletons going about everyday activities, devils, skulls, angels and various other characters can be seen, all made from papier mâché. Many of the sculptors are anonymous, but a few are well known. The late Pedro Linares, for example, was the head of a papier mâché making family, whose highly original work was collected by admirers including the painters Diego Rivera and Frida Kahlo. His family continues in this tradition, making amazing constructions, many hand-modelled without using moulds, of intricate figures of the dead or of symbolic animals, such as dragons or roosters.

Spain is another contemporary stronghold of papier mâché production, where enormous papier mâché characters with huge heads join the religious processions at Corpus Christi, and are later blown up with fireworks.

The craft of papier mâché has recently undergone a huge revival of interest in

Europe and America. This could be because of the current interest in recycling waste paper, the relative low cost and availability of the material, the ease with which the basic skills can be learned, or simply an appreciation of the vitality, versatility and beauty of the medium.

Whatever the reason, this simple material – paper – has inspired ancient and contemporary designers to produce exciting and original work and it looks set to continue well into the 21st century.

Above: A stunning papier mâché dragon or "alebrije" made by the Mexican Felipe Linares, using flour and water paste and a layering process. It is entirely hand-formed.

Left: Death Figure in a Purple Cape by Saulo Moreno, Mexico. This piece is entirely hand-formed, without using a mould. The modelling and detail is intricate and realistic.

GALLERY

PAPIER MACHE IS A VERY POPULAR MEDIUM AMONG CONTEMPORARY ARTISTS AND CRAFTSPEOPLE DUE TO ITS STRENGTH, ITS RELATIVE LOW COST AND THE EASE WITH WHICH IT CAN BE MOULDED INTO A MULTITUDE OF SHAPES. DRAWING ON INFLUENCES ANCIENT AND MODERN, THE INGENUITY AND SKILL OF THE CREATIVE ARTISTS REPRESENTED HERE HAS TRANSFORMED THIS HUMBLE TECHNIQUE INTO A STYLISH AND MODERN MEDIUM.

Right: BIRD SHRINES
These elegantly shaped shrines are inspired by the natural history displays found in museums. The case is constructed from papier mâché and contains a real bird's skull and a quail's egg. Both shrines include a small papier mâché bird inspired by illustrations from a book of 19th-century natural history engravings.
CAROLINE WAITE

Left: WHITE ICON
An innovative card construction covered with papier mâché. The surface of the case is decorated with a distressed paint surface, simulating an aged plaster wall, and embellished with real shells. The case contains a 19th-century porcelain doll, flanked by two flowers in vases.
CAROLINE WAITE

Left: SUN BOWL
This delicate sun-shaped bowl was made by layering handmade and recycled papers into a mould. A spiral of copper wire was added to each "petal" around the rim. Dried leaves were laid over the interior and exterior.
CLAIRE ATTRIDGE

Above: GOLDEN STAR FRUIT BOWL
This bowl was made by layering strips of paper into an existing fruit bowl mould. Geometric motifs and stars were painted in gold, complementing the rich purple and pink hues of the background.
HANNAH DOWNES

Left: RASPBERRY BOX
The intense colour of this casket is achieved by applying hand-coloured paper over a card armature. The box's bronze feet and the knob on the lid are gilded wooden balls, and the heart-shaped finial is formed from twists of copper wire.
CLAIRE ATTRIDGE

Left: LEAF BOWL
The main body of this small, textured bowl is constructed from layers of handmade and hand-coloured papers. Leaf skeletons stand out in low relief against the interior. A delicate filigree effect around the rim is achieved with twisted copper wire.
CLAIRE ATTRIDGE

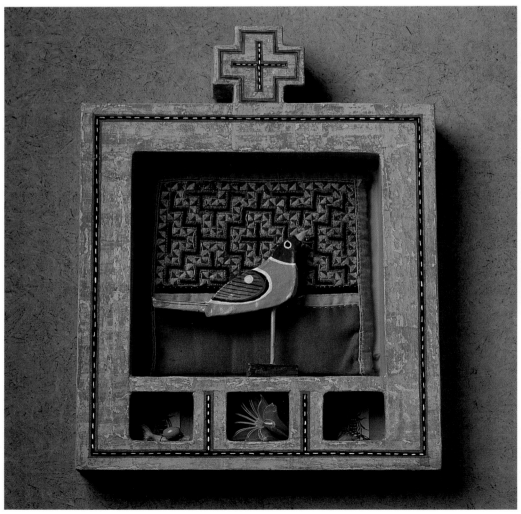

Left: BIRD WALL PANEL
Old fragments of richly embroidered cloth from Thailand were used as a background to this innovative wall panel. The bird and exterior structure are both constructed from papier mâché. Found objects have been placed in the three recesses at the bottom.
CAROLINE WAITE

Above: HOUSE OF DOLLS
An unusual display case housing an eccentric collection of dolls, created from buttons, jewels and doll parts, bound together with papier mâché. The dolls are dècorated with newspaper collage. Each doll is fitted with a brooch back so that it can be worn as jewellery, if desired.
JULIE ARKELL

Left: ELEGANT CASKETS
Recycled card and paper were used to construct the basic armatures for these caskets. Their elegance is created through a subtle combination of restrained background colours with gold embellishments. Bronze wire and gilded balls form the handles.
CLAIRE ATTRIDGE

Left: WALL BOX
A small door conceals a secret compartment lined with delicately patterned wallpaper, containing a red papier mâché heart. The box has a distressed background, adorned with bright painted symbols and a blossoming flower. An antique button is used as a small handle for the door.
CAROLINE WAITE

Above: GILDED PLATTERS AND BOWL
These decorative dishes demonstrate the versatility of papier mâché. Formed from plate and bowl moulds, the basecoat paint was slightly distressed with fine sandpaper before a layer of gold paint was applied, giving the impression of opulent gold leaf.
HANNAH DOWNES

MATERIALS

MANY OF THE MATERIALS NEEDED FOR PAPIER MACHE ARE INEXPENSIVE AND EASY TO OBTAIN. MAKING PAPIER MACHE IS A GREAT WAY OF RECYCLING MATERIALS, AND IT IS A GOOD IDEA TO SAVE NEWSPAPERS, OLD GREETINGS CARDS AND PAPERS, READY FOR USE IN PROJECTS. AVOID GLOSSY, WAXED OR LAMINATED SURFACES ON PAPERS WHICH ARE HARD TO MANIPULATE AND NON-POROUS, SO WILL NOT ABSORB GLUE.

Newspaper or newsprint (the raw paper) comes in different weights and qualities; broadsheets are usually printed on finer-quality newsprint than tabloids, and are strong and pliable, so ideal for layering into moulds and on to armatures. Tabloid newsprint is generally more porous and disintegrates readily when wet, so it is useful for making pulped details. Coloured sheets are helpful when building layers.

Corrugated cardboard also comes in different weights. "Double wall" cardboard has two rows of corrugations. This heavy-weight cardboard is ideal for making armatures that can be covered with layered strips to form a strong base. Boxes from electrical equipment are an ideal source. Single wall, or lightweight, corrugated card is good for low-relief details, such as moulding. Corrugated cardboard should be primed with a coat of diluted non-toxic PVA (white) glue and left to dry before the paper is applied, to minimize the risk of warping.

PVA (white) glue is ideal for making papier mâché, because it dries to a strong finish. It can be used undiluted to glue armatures, or diluted with water to the consistency of single cream to apply paper strips. PVA (white) dries clear and shiny, so it can also serve as a non-waterproof varnish for finished items. Always choose a non-toxic, and child-safe brand as some brands may irritate your skin. If you have sensitive skin, rub a barrier cream into your skin before using. As an extra precaution, apply the glue with a brush, or wear thin rubber (latex) gloves.

Water-based paste is also suitable, but takes longer to dry than PVA (white) glue. Do not be tempted to use wallpaper paste for papier mâché, as many brands contain fungicides, and should not come into prolonged contact with the skin. Non-toxic granules are the safest.

Tissue paper is ideal for making pulp. Soaked briefly in glue and squeezed out, it breaks down into a pulp that is easy to manipulate. For layering, tissue paper is very difficult to handle when wet as it disintegrates quickly; however, its stunning effects make it worth persevering with.

Recycled paper comes in all colours and textures. It can be used to make whole objects or used as a decorative layer over newspaper. Unlike newsprint, it generally has no grain, and so it is difficult to tear it into strips; the resulting papier mâché is therefore less regular.

Paint is used to prime work. Use two coats of non-toxic white paint to seal the surface and cover the print. Water-based paints, such as acrylic, emulsion (latex), poster and gouache are all suitable top coats. Papier mâché can also be gilded; prime first with two coats of acrylic gesso.

Varnish can be used to seal surfaces. A low-solvent polyurethane varnish is suitable over poster or gouache paints. Apply it in a well-ventilated area. Artist's aerosol varnishes can be used; wear a protective face mask when using these. If you have decorated with acrylic paints, protect with a water-based acrylic varnish.

Paper pulp can be made by shredding and soaking paper, but this is a long process. To make pulp mix rehydrated, store-bought pulp with undiluted PVA (white) glue to a thick paste. Add a filler of whiting (powdered chalk) to thicken. Pulp should be fairly stiff, without being too dry. Always wear a protective face mask and rubber (latex) gloves when preparing and handling pulp.

Wire mesh is useful for making shaped armatures. Fine-gauge wire mesh and chicken wire are the most common. Protective leather gloves are a must when handling the wire. When you cut out a shape, check the edges and remove any sharp spurs, disposing of them safely.

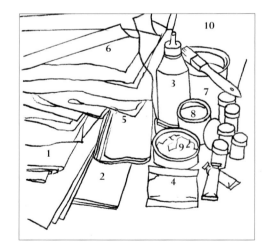

KEY

1 Newspaper	**6** Recycled paper
2 Corrugated cardboard	**7** Paint
3 PVA (white) glue	**8** Varnish
4 Water-based paste	**9** Paper pulp
5 Tissue paper	**10** Wire mesh

EQUIPMENT

PAPIER MACHE CAN BE MESSY, SO IT IS A GOOD IDEA TO COVER YOUR WORK SURFACE WITH A SHEET OF POLYTHENE OR HEAVY PLASTIC BEFORE YOU BEGIN. PROTECT YOUR CLOTHES TOO, WITH AN APRON OR OVERALL (SMOCK). YOU MAY FIND THAT YOU HAVE MANY ITEMS OF EQUIPMENT NEEDED TO MAKE PAPIER MACHE IN YOUR KITCHEN ALREADY. IF YOU ARE USING HOUSEHOLD PLATES AND BOWLS, BE SURE TO KEEP THEM FOR CRAFT PURPOSES ONLY.

Moulds Old plates are ideal moulds provided that no part of the interior of the mould is wider than the opening through which the papier mâché is to be removed. Balloons are perfect for round shapes; they can be popped with a pin before removal from the dry paper shell. Kitchen items used should not be re-used for food.

Petroleum jelly Grease moulds with a thin layer of petroleum jelly before use, so that the dry papier mâché can easily be removed. Cling film (plastic wrap) is a good alternative for flat surfaces.

Cutting mat Used to protect your surfaces from a sharp craft knife. Special mats can be bought from art supply shops. A thick sheet of plywood is a low-cost, less-permanent alternative.

Craft knife A craft knife is useful for cutting sheets of corrugated cardboard. Most knives have detachable blades, and some have a swivel head to cut out complex shapes with ease. All craft knives are extremely sharp, so it is important always to cut away from your body, and to keep the knife out of the reach of children.

Metal ruler A metal ruler will stand up to a sharp knife, and should be used for accurate cutting.

Scissors These are generally useful.

Masking tape This is a removable paper tape. It is useful for holding glued items in place while they dry. It also secures armatures while papier mâché is applied.

Paintbrushes A 2.5 cm (1 in) paintbrush is ideal for priming and applying varnish, as it covers a large area quickly. Buy a good-quality brush; cheaper brushes will shed hairs, ruining a smooth surface. Sable, sable/nylon, or nylon designer's brushes – flat or pointed – are suitable for decorating papier mâché with gouache or poster paints. Bristle brushes are suitable for applying acrylic paint. Wash, dry and store brushes carefully after use to keep them in good condition.

Fine sandpaper This is used to smooth the surface of dry papier mâché before it is primed. Sanding produces a fine dust, so always protect your face with a mask.

Wire cake rack This is used to support items as they dry. It speeds up the drying time by allowing air to circulate.

Bradawl A bradawl is a metal point mounted in a wooden handle used for piercing holes. Place the object on a scrap of wood before you pierce it, as the bradawl is very sharp. Stick the point of the bradawl into a cork when it is not in use, to keep it safe.

Leather gloves To protect the hands and wrists. Wear them when using materials such as wire mesh and chicken wire.

Rubber (latex) gloves Lightweight, close-fitting gloves should always be worn when using any form of adhesive and pulp.

Wire cutters These are used to clip through wire and wire mesh. A pair with a spring fulcrum is easier to use.

Protective mask A respiratory mask should always be worn when sanding, using powdered materials, and handling paper pulp, to prevent the inhalation of dust. A mask that protects against fumes should be used when working with strong-smelling glues and solvent-based products.

Modelling tool Modelling tools are useful for shaping paper pulp and come in many shapes and widths. Plastic and wooden versions are available from craft, sculptors' and potters' suppliers.

Palette A china palette, with separate compartments, is good for mixing small quantities of paint. An old, white china saucer makes a suitable substitute when no longer needed for food.

Pencil A pencil is needed for marking measurements and guidelines for cuttings.

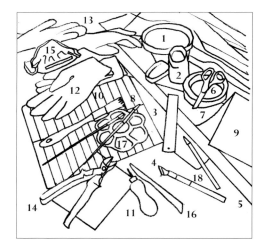

KEY

1 Mould
2 Petroleum jelly
3 Cutting mat
4 Craft knife
5 Metal ruler
6 Scissors
7 Masking tape
8 Paintbrushes
9 Fine sandpaper

10 Wire cake rack
11 Bradawl
12 Leather gloves
13 Rubber (latex) gloves
14 Wire cutters
15 Protective mask
16 Modelling tool
17 Palette
18 Pencil

BASIC TECHNIQUES

THERE ARE ONLY A FEW TECHNIQUES TO MASTER WHEN MAKING PAPIER MACHE BUT CARE IS NEEDED TO PRODUCE GOOD RESULTS. THE FINISHED SURFACE OF THE MATERIAL IS ALL-IMPORTANT, AND IT TAKES PRACTICE TO ACHIEVE A NEAT, REGULAR APPEARANCE. HOWEVER, ONCE YOU HAVE LEARNED THE BASIC SKILLS, YOU WILL PROBABLY DEVELOP YOUR OWN WAY OF WORKING, AND WILL PREFER SOME TYPES OF PAPER OR GLUE TO OTHERS.

TEARING NEWSPAPER

1 Tearing rather than cutting newspaper creates less obvious joins between strips. Like fabric, newspaper has a grain and will tear much more easily in one direction than the other. Generally, the grain runs from the top to the bottom of the newspaper. To make paper strips, grasp several folded sheets of newspaper in one hand, and begin a tear about 2.5 cm (1 in) from the edge. Pull directly down, and the paper will tear into long, straight strips. Strips of almost any width can be produced in this way.

2 If you try to tear newspaper across its width, you will be working against the grain, and the paper will be almost impossible to control. Find the grain by making a small tear in the top corner; if it is difficult to achieve this initial tear, turn the newspaper around!

PREPARING A MOULD

Before papier mâché is applied to it, the surface of the mould must be lightly greased with petroleum jelly, rather like a cake tin (pan). This will create a barrier between the glue and the mould, and prevent the papier mâché from sticking to it. It will then be easy to remove when it has dried. A piece of cling film (plastic wrap) can sometimes be used instead.

LAYERING INTO A MOULD

Large moulds, such as plates and bowls, can be covered using paper strips approximately 2.5 cm (1 in) wide. Five to six layers should suffice. Spread the strips with glue on both sides and lay them in the greased mould. They should be slightly longer than the mould and protrude beyond the edge, so that the whole area is covered. Smooth each strip gently with your fingers and press out any air bubbles under the paper. Each new strip should slightly overlap the last to give a really strong result.

MAKING CARDBOARD ARMATURES

1 To build three-dimensional items without using a mould, make an armature from heavy corrugated cardboard and cover with papier mâché. The cardboard becomes a permanent part of the structure. Measure each piece of the armature carefully, and glue and tape in place to create a sturdy and durable framework.

2 Brush the armature with a coat of diluted PVA (white) glue and leave to dry before applying paper strips or pulp. This will seal the surface of the cardboard, making it less absorbent and preventing it from warping once the strips of glued paper are added.

3 Cover the sealed armature with papier mâché in the usual way. Approximately five layers of paper will make a strong object and disguise the corrugated cardboard underneath. Apply each layer of strips at right angles to the layer beneath for extra strength.

4 When the layers of papier mâché are complete, leave the armature to dry overnight – or longer in cold weather. Place the object on a wire cake rack in a warm, dry place. Do not be tempted to speed up the drying by setting the item close to direct heat, which could warp the papier mâché and the framework.

PREPARING THE SURFACE

1 All papier mâché should be prepared properly if you intend to paint it, especially if it is made from newspaper. First, rub the surface with fine sandpaper to smooth it and disguise the edges of the paper strips. Remember to wear a protective face mask when sanding.

2 Prime the papier mâché with two coats of non-toxic paint. This provides a good ground for paint, and conceals the newsprint. Emulsion (latex) paint is ideal, but poster or powder paint also works well. Acrylic paint is suitable if the subseqent decoration is done with acrylic.

PROTECTING YOUR SKIN

1 Before making papier mâché, it is advisable to rub a thin covering of petroleum jelly or rich moisturizer into your hands. This will protect your hands from dryness and make it much easier to clean your hands when you have finished, especially if you use PVA (white) glue.

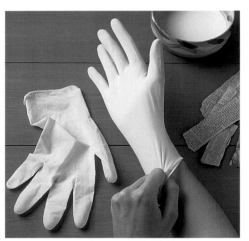

2 Although you should always use non-toxic, fungicide-free glues and pastes, wear a pair of thin rubber (latex) gloves when handling contact adhesive and pulp, and at other times if your skin is sensitive. Do not make papier mâché if you have a skin condition or broken skin.

DRYING FLAT OBJECTS

Objects such as frames and wall panels should be dried flat after sealing and when covered with papier mâché, to prevent warping. Place the object on a wire cake rack or a sheet of thin plastic. Although the glue will stick to the plastic as it dries, the plastic can easily be peeled away once the item is dry.

CUTTING CARDBOARD WITH A RULER

Always use a metal ruler or straight edge and a cutting mat when working with a craft knife. Plastic rulers are not sturdy enough to withstand sharp blades, and will develop nicks along their edges, becoming unusable.

CURVING CORRUGATED CARDBOARD

1 Scoring enables corrugated cardboard to be formed into all sorts of curved shapes. Cut a strip to the required size, making sure that the corrugations run from top to bottom of the shape. Use a craft knife to carefully score down each concave corrugation.

2 When all the score lines have been made, the cardboard will be flexible enough to curve into a variety of shapes.

MAKING PAPER PULP

Always wear a protective face mask and thin rubber (latex) gloves, when making paper pulp. Mix rehydrated paper pulp and PVA (white) glue in a container to a thick paste. Sieve whiting (powdered chalk) into the mixture until it is malleable, but not too stiff or too dry.

KALEIDOSCOPIC ROOM DIVIDER

THIS COLOURFUL DIVIDER IS MADE BY LAYERING SIMPLE TISSUE PAPER SHAPES TO CREATE A TRANSLUCENT, KALEIDOSCOPIC EFFECT. EACH SECTION IS FORMED AS A SEPARATE SQUARE, THEN STITCHED TO A BACKGROUND OF JAPANESE HAND-LAID PAPER, WHICH IS SHEER BUT INCREDIBLY STRONG. SEEN AGAINST DAY-LIGHT, THE TRANSLUCENT TISSUE PAPER IS HEIGHTENED, AND THE COLOURS GLOW WITH A VIVID INTENSITY. THE DESIGNS MUST BE SIMPLE FOR THE GREATEST IMPACT; COMPLICATED PATTERNS CAN LOOK TOO BUSY. AS WATER-BASED GLUE IS USED, IT IS IMPORTANT TO CHOOSE BLEEDPROOF TISSUE PAPER, OR THE COLOURS WILL RUN.

1 Cut the required number of backing squares measuring 36 x 36 cm (14 x 14 in) from white tissue paper. Cut a range of coloured tissue paper shapes.

3 When the squares are thoroughly dry, gently peel them from the plastic. Place each one on a cutting mat and carefully trim the edges.

5 Trim the handmade paper to size if necessary, then glue the sheets together using undiluted PVA (white) glue to make the screen as wide and long as necessary.

2 Place a white square on a sheet of plastic. Lay the coloured shapes on top according to the design. Brush diluted PVA (white) glue over the square and apply the first layer of shapes. Build up the design, adding layers. Leave the square to dry. Repeat to decorate the other squares.

4 Place the paper squares in position on the sheets of handmade paper, making sure that they are evenly spaced. Pin the squares to the paper and machine- or hand-stitch them in place, removing the pins before you get to them.

6 Fold over 2.5 cm (1 in) of paper to the back of the screen and crease it into place. Stitch along the edge of the fold to make a casing for a length of dowel, so that the screen can be suspended.

MATERIALS AND EQUIPMENT YOU WILL NEED

BLEEDPROOF TISSUE PAPER, WHITE AND VARIETY OF COLOURS • ZIG-ZAG OR ORDINARY SCISSORS •
SHEET OF PLASTIC • NON-TOXIC PVA (WHITE) GLUE • PAINTBRUSH • CRAFT KNIFE AND CUTTING MAT • METAL RULER •
HANDMADE JAPANESE PAPER • DRESSMAKING PINS • SEWING THREAD AND NEEDLE • SEWING MACHINE (OPTIONAL) • LENGTH OF DOWEL

MEXICAN CARNIVAL DOLL

THIS DOLL IS MADE ENTIRELY FROM PAPER PULP, WHICH DRIES TO A VERY HARD FINISH. HER ARMS AND LEGS ARE PIERCED, AND THE JOINTS MADE WITH PIPE CLEANERS, ALLOWING HER TO MOVE HER LIMBS. PULP IS HERE MOULDED BY HAND USING THE SAME TECHNIQUE USED FOR MOULDING CLAY. BEFORE THE DOLL IS PAINTED, ALL THE PIECES ARE SANDED CAREFULLY TO MAKE THEM COMPLETELY SMOOTH. THIS PROVIDES A LOVELY SURFACE TO PAINT ON, AND GIVES THE PULP THE APPEARANCE OF PORCELAIN. IT SHOULD BE NOTED THAT THIS DOLL IS NOT A TOY, AND IS NOT SUITABLE FOR CHILDREN.

1 Wearing rubber (latex) gloves and a face mask, form the doll's torso and head from a sausage of paper pulp. Make the head by gently pulling a blob of pulp up out of the main mass of the body. Bend a length of thin galvanized wire into a U shape and push it down through the head into the body to strengthen the doll.

2 Use small pellets of pulp to mould the doll's hair and cover up the wire. Allow the doll's body to dry slightly, then place it on a scrap of wood, and gently make a channel through the shoulders and hips with a bradawl. Leave it on an old wire cake rack to dry.

3 Model two arms and legs from pulp. When they have dried out slightly, use a bradawl to make a hole through the top of each limb so that they can be joined to the doll's body. Leave the limbs on the rack to dry completely.

▶

MATERIALS AND EQUIPMENT YOU WILL NEED

THIN RUBBER (LATEX) GLOVES • PROTECTIVE FACE MASK • PAPER PULP (SEE BASIC TECHNIQUES) • THIN GALVANIZED WIRE • WIRE CUTTERS • BRADAWL • SCRAP OF WOOD • OLD WIRE CAKE RACK • FINE SANDPAPER • NON-TOXIC WHITE ACRYLIC GESSO • PAINTBRUSHES • NON-TOXIC ACRYLIC PAINTS IN A VARIETY OF COLOURS • WATER-BASED MATT ACRYLIC VARNISH • PIPE CLEANERS

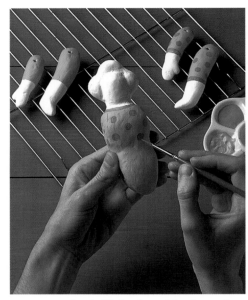

4 When all the pieces of the doll are completely dry, smooth their surfaces with fine sandpaper. Smooth until the pieces resemble fine porcelain. Wear a protective face mask while sanding.

6 Paint the doll's body and limbs with yellow acrylic paint. Add bands of orange around the wrists, ankles and neck, and paint orange spots over the yellow background.

7 Use a fine paintbrush to depict the doll's features. Paint her hair and boots black. When the doll is completely dry, seal the surface with two coats of water-based matt acrylic varnish.

5 Prime the doll's body and limbs with two coats of white acrylic gesso. Allow the first coat to dry thoroughly before applying the second. Leave to dry completely on the wire cake rack.

8 Place the doll flat, and position the arms and legs. Push pipe cleaners all the way through the arms and legs and the body, and twist the ends to keep the limbs securely in place.

GRECIAN VASE

THIS LONG-NECKED VASE IS BASED ON THE VESSELS PRODUCED IN THE MEDITERRANEAN AREA SINCE ANCIENT TIMES. ITS DESIGN IS A GOOD EXAMPLE OF HOW THE HUMBLEST OF OBJECTS — TWO YOGURT POTS AND A BALLOON — CAN BE THE BASIS FOR STYLISH PAPIER MACHE. A FINAL LAYER OF BROWN WRAPPING PAPER SHOWS THROUGH THE CHALKY PAINT TO REINFORCE THE SUN-BLEACHED, MEDITERRANEAN THEME. TWO LENGTHS OF CURVED DRIFTWOOD FORM THE VASE HANDLES, AND A SHELL WASHED SMOOTH AND PIERCED BY THE SEA, LEND AN APPROPRIATE FINISHING TOUCH.

1 Inflate a round balloon and tie the end firmly. Rest the balloon on a small bowl. Tear newspaper into 2.5 cm (1 in) wide strips and dip them into the diluted PVA (white) glue. Cover the balloon with 5–6 layers of papier mâché strips, making sure that it is evenly coated. Suspend the balloon from a length of string to dry.

2 Cut two lengths of cord long enough to fit around the necks of the yogurt containers. Wind the cord around the tops of the containers and keep it in place with small strips of masking tape. Turn the containers upside down and carefully cut out the base of each one, using scissors.

3 Tear some more 2.5 cm (1 in) strips of newspaper. Dip the strips into the diluted PVA (white) glue, and cover each container with three layers. Use thin strips to bind the rims of the containers so that the cord is neatly covered. Leave the containers to dry completely. ▶

MATERIALS AND EQUIPMENT YOU WILL NEED

ROUND BALLOON • SMALL BOWL • NEWSPAPER • NON-TOXIC DILUTED PVA (WHITE) GLUE • STRING • SCISSORS • COTTON CORD •
TWO CLEAN, DRY YOGURT CONTAINERS OF DIFFERENT SIZES • MASKING TAPE • PIN • PENCIL • BROWN WRAPPING PAPER •
PROTECTIVE FACE MASK • FINE SANDPAPER • NON-TOXIC WHITE EMULSION (LATEX) PAINT • SAND AND FILLING PLASTER • BROAD PAINTBRUSH •
STRONG, CLEAR GLUE • TWO PIECES OF CURVED DRIFTWOOD • HAIRY TWINE • WORN SHELL OR PEBBLE

4 When the papier mâché on the balloon is completely dry, pierce with a pin to pop the balloon within. Position the paper shape centrally on the smaller yogurt container and hold it in place with strips of masking tape. Cover the join with several layers of thin papier mâché strips.

5 Position the larger tub centrally on top of the paper shape. Draw around the inside of the container and carefully cut away the resulting circle to make the opening of the vase. Replace the container and tape it in place. Cover the join with several layers of papier mâché.

6 When dry, tear some large strips of brown wrapping paper, dip them into the diluted PVA (white) glue, and apply one layer to the vase. Leave the vase to dry thoroughly. Then, wearing a protective face mask, lightly sand the surface.

7 Wearing a protective face mask, mix some white emulsion (latex) paint with a little sand and filling plaster. Use a broad brush to paint the vase, including the inside of the neck. Allow the brown paper to show through in some areas, to give the vase a slightly patchy appearance. Leave the vase to dry thoroughly.

8 Wind hairy twine around the neck and foot of the vase. Suspend a piece of worn shell or pebble from a length of twine to adorn the neck of the vase.

9 Using strong, clear glue, attach a length of driftwood to either side of the vase to form the handles. Secure them in place with masking tape while they dry.

BIRD'S-FOOT TABLE LAMP

THIS SPIKY LAMP-STAND IS MADE ON A WIRE ARMATURE GLUED AROUND A THREADED METAL CORE. PAPIER MACHE STRIPS COVER THE WIRE, AND THE LIGHT FITTINGS ARE ATTACHED TO THE TOP OF THE CORE. WHITE PAINT GIVES THE LAMP BASE A CONTEMPORARY LOOK AND WILL COORDINATE WITH A SHADE OF ANY COLOUR. MAKE SURE THAT YOUR LAMP BASE IS COMPLETELY STABLE; IF IN DOUBT, MOUNT THE FEET ON A BLOCK OF PAINTED WOOD USING U-PINS.

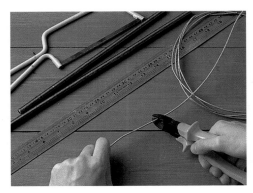

1 Use wire cutters to cut four pieces of galvanized wire, each measuring 91 cm (36 in) long. Clamp the threaded core firmly in a vice, and saw a length measuring 35 cm (14 in).

2 Gently bend each length of wire in half. Measure 11 cm (4½ in) in from the ends of the wire and bend the ends outward at this point to form the feet of the lamp.

3 Use epoxy resin glue to attach the wire strips to the metal core and bind with masking tape.

4 Bind the ends of each foot together with strips of masking tape. Place the stand upright and make sure that it is stable, adjusting the position of the feet as necessary. Screw the lamp fitting to the top of the metal core.

5 Apply two layers of papier mâché strips to the stand, avoiding the light fitting, and smoothing them over the shape of the wire. Leave to dry.

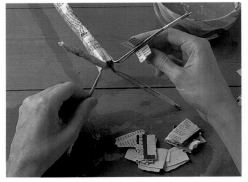

6 Cover the feet in several layers of paper. Dry, and coat twice with white paint, avoiding the light fitting. If the base needs to be stabilized, attach the stand to a block of wood using U-pins. Ask an electrician to wire the lamp base.

MATERIALS AND EQUIPMENT YOU WILL NEED

WIRE CUTTERS • 2 MM (1/16 IN) GALVANIZED WIRE • THREADED METAL CORE • HACKSAW • WORK BENCH AND VICE • EPOXY RESIN GLUE • MASKING TAPE • SCISSORS • LAMP FITTING • NEWSPAPER • NON-TOXIC PASTE • PAINTBRUSHES • NON-TOXIC WHITE EMULSION (LATEX) PAINT • BLOCK OF WOOD (OPTIONAL) • U-PINS AND TACK HAMMER (OPTIONAL)

LEAFY WALL PANELS

PAPIER MACHE PANELS AND OTHER ARCHITECTURAL DETAILS WERE POPULAR DURING THE 19TH CENTURY, WHEN ELABORATE IMITATIONS OF PLASTER- AND STUCCOWORK WERE PRODUCED. THESE PANELS ARE LESS ORNATE THAN THEIR PREDECESSORS, BUT WILL ADD A TOUCH OF ELEGANCE AROUND A DOOR FRAME. THE SURFACE IS RUBBED BACK WITH FINE SANDPAPER TO REVEAL JUST A HINT OF UNDERLYING COLOUR, GIVING THE DESIGN SUBTLE DEFINITION. THE PANELS MAY BE TEMPORARILY ATTACHED, USING STICKY PADS OR, FOR MORE PERMANENT DECORATION, USE UNDILUTED PVA (WHITE) GLUE.

1 For the side and top of the door, cut three panels of cardboard measuring 60 x 14 cm (24 x 5½ in), or to fit around your door. Brush both sides of each panel with a coat of diluted PVA (white) glue and lay flat on a sheet of plastic to dry.

2 Draw a line down the centre of each panel. Measure and mark a point every 15 cm (6 in) down the line.

3 Dab a spot of undiluted PVA (white) glue at each 15 cm (6 in) mark. Cut a length of cotton cord for each panel, and attach in a wavy line, curving it in and out between the dabs of glue. Use small pieces of masking tape to keep the cord in place. Line the panels up, end to end, to make sure that the ends of the cords form a continuous wavy pattern.

4 Trace the leaf motif from the template at the back of the book, and transfer it four times to a piece of heavy corrugated cardboard for each panel. Place the cardboard on a cutting mat and cut out all the leaves, using a craft knife. Glue the leaves at equal distances down the length of each panel. Tear newspaper into 2.5 cm (1 in) strips, dip them in diluted PVA (white) glue, and cover each panel with three layers. Lay the panels flat on a sheet of plastic to dry. ▶

MATERIALS AND EQUIPMENT YOU WILL NEED

HEAVY CORRUGATED CARDBOARD • SCISSORS • NON-TOXIC PVA (WHITE) GLUE • PAINTBRUSHES • SHEET OF PLASTIC • METAL RULER • PENCIL • THICK COTTON CORD • MASKING TAPE • TRACING PAPER • CRAFT KNIFE AND CUTTING MAT • NEWSPAPER • PROTECTIVE FACE MASK • FINE SANDPAPER • NON-TOXIC EMULSION (LATEX) PAINTS: WHITE AND BLUE • SOFT CLOTH • PETROLEUM JELLY • STICKY PADS (OPTIONAL)

5 Wearing a protective face mask, gently rub down each panel with fine sandpaper to smooth it. Prime the panels with two coats of white emulsion (latex) paint and leave to dry thoroughly.

7 Using a soft cloth, apply a very thin coat of petroleum jelly over the front of each panel.

8 Paint each panel with two coats of white emulsion (latex) paint, completely covering the blue surface. Leave the panels to dry thoroughly.

6 Still wearing the protective face mask, paint the front of each panel with a coat of blue emulsion (latex) paint. Leave them to dry thoroughly.

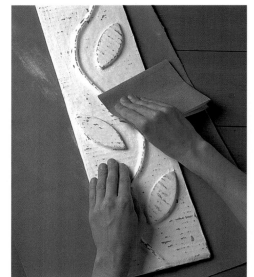

9 Again wearing a mask, rub down the surface of each panel very lightly, using fine sandpaper, so that specks of blue paint are revealed. Attach the panels around the door frame, using PVA (white) glue, or sticky pads if temporary.

KEEPSAKE BOX

THIS BOX MAKES A CHARMING HIDING PLACE FOR TREASURED ITEMS. ITS SOPHISTICATED APPEARANCE BELIES ITS SIMPLE CONSTRUCTION; IT IS STRAIGHTFORWARD TO MAKE, BUT THE ELEMENTS MUST BE PRECISELY MEASURED AND CUT TO ENSURE A PERFECT FIT. THE DELICATE, SLIGHTLY WEATHERED SURFACE IS ACHIEVED BY PAINTING WITH THREE DIFFERENT COLOURS, OVERLAID AND RUBBED BACK TO CREATE A PATCHY, AGED EFFECT. SUBTLE PAINTED MOTIFS AND COLLAGED SCRAPS ENHANCE THE LOOK, AND PROVIDE AN OPPORTUNITY TO PERSONALIZE THE BOX.

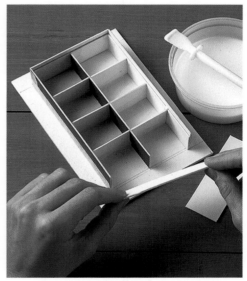

1 For the base of the box, cut two pieces of mounting board measuring 11.5 x 16.5 cm (4½ x 6½ in), and glue them together. Measure and mark out the positions of the box walls and compartments as follows: Draw a rectangle 1.5 cm (⅝ in) from the edges of the base. Draw a second rectangle inside it that is 2 mm (¹⁄₁₆ in) smaller all round. Divide this rectangle into eight equal sections for the compartments.

2 Cut three strips of mounting board measuring 13.5 x 2.5 cm (5¼ x 1 in). Using the PVA (white) glue, glue and tape one strip along the centre of the base. Glue and tape the other two strips along the edges of the inner rectangle. Cut two further strips of 2.5 cm (1 in) wide board to make the walls for the ends of the inner rectangle, and glue and tape one of these strips into place.

3 Cut four strips of 3 cm (1⅛ in) wide board to make walls for the larger rectangle. Glue and tape three strips in position, as before. Measure and cut eight pieces of 2.5 cm (1 in) wide board to make the compartments, and glue and tape them in place inside the central rectangle. Glue the remaining two board strips in place at the side of the box. ▶

MATERIALS AND EQUIPMENT YOU WILL NEED

A2 SHEET OF MOUNTING BOARD • METAL RULER, SET SQUARE AND PENCIL • CRAFT KNIFE AND CUTTING MAT • NON-TOXIC PVA (WHITE) GLUE •
MASKING TAPE • NEWSPAPER • NON-TOXIC PASTE • NON-TOXIC WHITE EMULSION (LATEX) PAINT • PAINTBRUSHES •
GOUACHE PAINTS IN A VARIETY OF COLOURS • PROTECTIVE FACE MASK • FINE SANDPAPER • SCRAPS OF INTERESTING PAPER •
MATT ACRYLIC VARNISH • ORNAMENTAL BUTTON

4 Cut four 3 cm (1⅛ in) wide strips of board to make the outer walls of the base, and glue and tape them into position. Cut four strips of board to fit over the space between the compartments and the outer walls, and glue and tape them into place.

6 Using a pencil and ruler, divide the top of the lid in four sections to find the central point. Cut a small rectangle of board to make a ledge for the button that forms the handle. Cut a small notch into the rectangle to contain the shank of the button.

8 Prime the box and lid with a coat of white emulsion (latex) paint. When dry, apply a coat of turquoise paint, mixed from gouache and white emulsion (latex). Follow this with a coat of lighter, blue-green paint, then one of yellow ochre. All the colours should be applied with a dry brush, and dry before the next is added. When the last coat is dry, lightly rub down the surface of the box and lid with fine sandpaper, wearing a face mask.

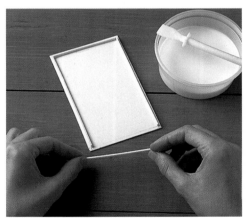

5 To make the lid, measure the opening in the top of the box and cut out two rectangles of mounting board that are 3 mm (⅛ in) smaller all round than the opening. Glue the rectangles together. Draw a line around the lid 2 mm (¹⁄₁₆ in) in from the edge. Cut four 3 mm (⅛ in) pieces of mounting board to fit inside the pencil line and glue them in place to make a lip for the lid.

7 Cover the entire box and lid with two layers of papier mâché squares, pasted smoothly over the surface. Leave the box and lid to dry thoroughly.

9 Paste scraps of paper on to the surface of the box and lid. Sketch decorative motifs faintly with a pencil, then fill in using gouache paints. When the box and lid are dry, seal them with a coat of acrylic varnish. Finally, glue the button to the top of the lid to make the handle.

those we love

STAR FRAME

THE WARM TONES OF BROWN WRAPPING PAPER MAKE IT IDEAL FOR PAPIER MACHE, EITHER ON ITS OWN, OR OVER NEWSPAPER. THIS FRAME, WITH ITS LOW-RELIEF PATTERN, EXPLOITS THE MATERIAL'S NATURAL QUALITIES IN A SIMPLE, HARMONIOUS DESIGN. BROWN PAPER IS LESS EASY TO HANDLE THAN NEWSPAPER; IT IS THICKER, AND MORE DIFFICULT TO TEAR INTO REGULAR STRIPS. THE TORN EDGES ALSO TEND TO DARKEN WHEN THE GLUE HAS DRIED, BUT THIS MAKES FOR A LIVELY, INTERESTING SURFACE. CHOOSE YOUR PAPER CAREFULLY, AS SOME ARE WAXED TO MAKE THEM WATERPROOF, AND ARE NOT SUITABLE FOR PAPIER MACHE.

1 Use a ruler and set square to draw a square, 38 x 38 cm (15 x 15 in), on to corrugated cardboard. Draw another square within it, measuring 18 x 18 cm (7 x 7 in), to make the frame opening. Place the cardboard on a cutting mat and cut out the frame with a craft knife.

2 Draw a star design and transfer it eight times to corrugated cardboard. Cut out all the stars.

3 Cut four small circles of cardboard and glue them to the centres of four of the stars. Glue all the stars around the frame, with the plain stars at the corners.

4 Measure and cut out a 38 x 38 cm (15 x 15 in) backing board from the cardboard. Draw and cut out a frame spacer from lightweight corrugated cardboard. Prime the frame front, back and spacer with diluted PVA (white) glue and place them flat on a sheet of plastic to dry.

5 Glue the spacer to the back of the frame. Tear wide strips of brown paper and dip into the diluted PVA (white) glue. Cover the frame and backing board with two layers. Lay flat to dry.

6 Glue the backing board to the back of the frame, lining up the edges. Hold the frame together with masking tape and seal the bottom and side edges with two layers of papier mâché strips. When dry, glue a hanger to the back with clear glue.

MATERIALS AND EQUIPMENT YOU WILL NEED

METAL RULER, SET SQUARE AND PENCIL • HEAVY CORRUGATED CARDBOARD • CRAFT KNIFE AND CUTTING MAT • TRACING PAPER • NON-TOXIC PVA (WHITE) GLUE • LIGHTWEIGHT CORRUGATED CARDBOARD, FOR SPACER • PAINTBRUSH • SHEET OF PLASTIC • BROWN WRAPPING PAPER • MASKING TAPE • STRONG, CLEAR GLUE • PICTURE HANGER

GILDED FINIALS

FINIALS CAN TRANSFORM EVERYDAY CURTAIN POLES INTO STYLISH ACCESSORIES. NO ONE WOULD GUESS THAT THESE GLISTENING EXAMPLES ARE MADE FROM FOAMBOARD, PULP TISSUE PAPER AND PLASTIC BOTTLE CAPS. THE GOLD IS DUTCH METAL LEAF (CHEAPER THAN GOLD LEAF), WHICH IS APPLIED IN SHEETS OVER A STICKY LIQUID CALLED SIZE. YOU CAN USE GOLD PAINT OR GILT CREAM INSTEAD, BUT THEY WILL NOT SPARKLE WITH THE SAME INTENSITY AS METAL LEAF.

1 Trace the finial design from the template, and transfer it twice to a piece of foamboard. Place the foamboard on a cutting mat and carefully cut out the finials using a craft knife.

2 Brush the finials on both sides with diluted PVA (white) glue and lay them flat on a wire cake rack to dry thoroughly.

3 Dip pieces of tissue paper into the diluted PVA (white) glue. Squeeze out the excess glue, and work the tissue paper lightly in your hands until it becomes pulpy. Press the pulp on to one side of the finial shapes and smooth the surface. Lay them flat on the cake rack to dry well. ▶

MATERIALS AND EQUIPMENT YOU WILL NEED

TRACING PAPER AND PENCIL • 5 MM (¼ IN) THICK FOAMBOARD • CRAFT KNIFE AND CUTTING MAT • NON-TOXIC PVA (WHITE) GLUE •
PAINTBRUSHES • OLD WIRE CAKE RACK • TISSUE PAPER • PLASTIC BOTTLE CAPS • STRONG, CLEAR GLUE • MASKING TAPE • NEWSPAPER •
PROTECTIVE FACE MASK • FINE SANDPAPER • WHITE ACRYLIC GESSO • WATER-BASED GOLD SIZE • LARGE SOFT BRUSH • GOLD DUTCH METAL LEAF

4 Draw around the top of a bottle cap twice on to the foamboard and cut out the resulting circles. Glue a circle to the base of each finial.

6 Tear narrow strips of newspaper, dip them into the diluted PVA (white) glue, and cover the dry finials with three layers of papier mâché. Leave the finials to dry thoroughly.

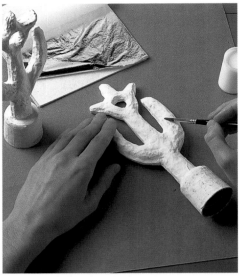

8 Apply a thin coat of water-based gold size to one finial and leave it to become tacky (about 20–30 minutes).

5 Glue the base of a finial to the top of each bottle cap, keeping them in place with small strips of masking tape.

7 Wearing a protective face mask, lightly sand each finial, and prime with two coats of white acrylic gesso. Allow the first coat to dry completely before the second coat is added.

9 Using a large, soft brush, apply metal leaf over the tacky gold size, continuing until the whole of the finial is covered. Brush away the excess leaf. Gild the second finial in the same way.

ROCOCO SCREEN

THIS ORNATE AND GRACEFUL SCREEN IS MADE USING THE SIMPLEST OF MATERIALS; THIN CORRUGATED CARDBOARD AND TISSUE PAPER, APPLIED TO A THREE-PANEL BLANK. THE OUTER EDGES CAN BE AS ELABORATE AS YOU LIKE, BUT THE DECORATIONS ON THE CENTRAL PANEL MUST FIT FLUSH TO THE EDGES TO ENABLE YOU TO HINGE THE SCREEN. THE BLANKS CAN BE PURCHASED FROM CRAFT AND HOBBY SHOPS, OR DIRECT FROM THE SUPPLIER, BY MAIL ORDER. YOU COULD, OF COURSE, CUT THEM YOURSELF, OR ASK YOUR LOCAL CARPENTER TO DO SO, GIVING YOU A SCREEN THAT FITS YOUR DESIGN SPECIFICATIONS EXACTLY.

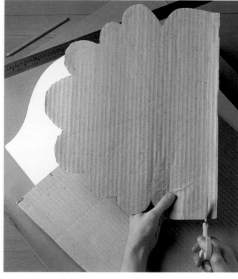

1 Wearing a protective face mask, lightly rub down both sides of each screen panel with fine sandpaper, then prime each one with acrylic primer.

2 Cut a large piece of thin corrugated cardboard to cover each screen panel. The cardboard for the central panel should fit exactly; the cardboard for the side panels should overlap by 6 cm (2½ in). Draw a fan-shaped section for the top of each panel and cut out.

3 Draw and cut out slender curlicues of cardboard. Position them down one side of the cardboard that will cover the outer panels. Draw around them in pencil, and cut around the outer lines to make the decorative edges of the panels. ▶

MATERIALS AND EQUIPMENT YOU WILL NEED

PROTECTIVE FACE MASK • THREE-PANEL SCREEN BLANK • FINE SANDPAPER • WATER-BASED ACRYLIC PRIMER • PAINTBRUSHES • SCISSORS • THIN CORRUGATED CARDBOARD WITH EXPOSED CORRUGATIONS • METAL RULER AND PENCIL • CRAFT KNIFE AND CUTTING MAT • THIN RUBBER (LATEX) GLOVES • CONTACT ADHESIVE • NON-TOXIC PVA (WHITE) GLUE • WHITE TISSUE PAPER • NON-TOXIC EMULSION (LATEX) PAINTS: WHITE AND A VARIETY OF PALE COLOURS • NON-TOXIC GOLD ACRYLIC PAINT • NON-TOXIC WATER-BASED ACRYLIC VARNISH • SET OF PIANO HINGES

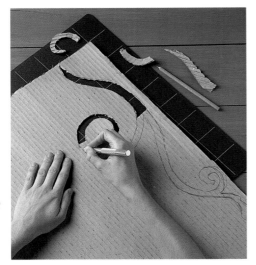

4 Use the curlicues as templates along the other edge of the side panels. This time, cut out the shapes, using a craft knife, to make indented patterns.

6 Cut smaller swirls and embellishments to fit around the top of each screen as a relief design. Fix them into position with PVA (white) glue. Stick the curlicues in place over the main panels of the screen.

7 When all the additions have dried, tear thick strips of tissue paper and apply two layers over the surface of all three panels, using diluted PVA (white) glue and a wide brush. Make sure that you cover the edges of the screen, to bond the panels firmly. Leave the panels to dry.

5 Wearing a protective face mask and thin rubber (latex) gloves, glue the cardboard to the panels, using the contact adhesive.

8 Prime the panels with white emulsion (latex) paint, then decorate them with pale shades of emulsion (latex) paint and gold outlines in acrylic paint. Seal the panels with two coats of acrylic varnish, and hinge the screen together.

PEBBLE CLOCK

Natural objects and everyday materials are charmingly combined in this clock to echo the passage of time. The basic armature is a disc of heavy corrugated cardboard, and the hours are picked out using slender pebbles, collected while beachcombing. A frill of short twigs makes a spiked contrast to the plain white rim of the clock face — short pieces of driftwood, shells or more pebbles would also look good. The clock is fitted with a quartz movement, available from craft suppliers or hobby shops, in a variety of styles and sizes.

1 To make the clock face, draw a circle with a diameter of 26 cm (10¼ in) on a sheet of heavy corrugated cardboard. Place the cardboard on a cutting mat, and cut out the circle with a craft knife.

2 Tear newspaper into 2.5 cm (1 in) strips and dip them in diluted PVA (white) glue. Cover the clock face with three layers of strips and lay it on a wire cake rack to dry thoroughly.

3 Using a sharp pencil, make a hole in the exact centre of the clock face wide enough for the clock movement to be inserted. Follow the manufacturer's instructions for operating the movement. ▶

MATERIALS AND EQUIPMENT YOU WILL NEED

PAIR OF COMPASSES AND PENCIL • HEAVY CORRUGATED CARDBOARD • CRAFT KNIFE AND CUTTING MAT • NEWSPAPER • NON-TOXIC PVA (WHITE) GLUE • OLD WIRE CAKE RACK • SHARP PENCIL • CLOCK MOVEMENT AND HANDS • PROTECTIVE FACE MASK • FINE SANDPAPER • NON-TOXIC WHITE EMULSION (LATEX) PAINT • PAINTBRUSH • SCISSORS • BROWN WRAPPING PAPER • MATT GOLD PAPER • STRONG, CLEAR GLUE • PEBBLES • THIN TWIGS

4 Wearing a protective face mask, lightly rub the surface of the clock face with fine sandpaper and prime it with two coats of white emulsion (latex) paint. Allow the first coat to dry thoroughly before applying the second.

6 Use the pencil to punch through the existing hole into the brown and gold paper. Fix the clock movement and hands to the clock face, following the manufacturer's instructions.

8 Cut the twigs into short lengths. Draw a guideline 2.5cm (1 in) from the edge of the clock. Working on the back of the clock, glue the twigs at equal distances around the edge. Place the clock face down and leave to dry thoroughly.

5 Cut a circle of brown paper with a diameter of 25 cm (10 in), and a circle of matt gold paper with a diameter of 9 cm (3½ in). Glue both to the centre of the clock face.

7 Turn the hands to 12 o'clock and make a corresponding pencil mark on the clock face. Rotate the hands and mark each hour in the border.

9 Turn the clock over and use strong, clear glue to attach a pebble at each hour mark on the clock face. Cut very short lengths of twig and glue them around the edge of the inner, gold circle. Lay the clock flat until the glue is thoroughly dry.

STARRY DRAWER KNOBS

Decorative knobs can enliven the plainest door or drawer. These star drawer knobs are made entirely from pulp tissue paper, but are very strong when dry. A machine screw fixes them to the drawer. They are simply finished with spirals of household string, and a touch of gold paint to emphasize their shape. Drawer knobs offer a wide scope for embellishing plain cupboards: you could make a set of door knobs, using a different motif for each, or try using coloured tissue paper as a final layer, and leave the drawers unpainted.

1 Loosely crumple a sheet of tissue paper into a ball and dip it into diluted PVA (white) glue until completely saturated.

2 Squeeze the excess glue from the paper and work it between your hands for a few seconds, so that it breaks down and becomes pulpy. Form the pulp into a small ball.

3 To make each knob, hold a ball of pulp between your thumbs and forefingers and flatten it into a disc. Gently press the disc between your fingers until the paper is completely smooth. Place the disc on a wire rack to dry slightly. Repeat to make as many knobs as you need. ▶

MATERIALS AND EQUIPMENT YOU WILL NEED

TISSUE PAPER • NON-TOXIC PVA (WHITE) GLUE • WIRE CAKE RACK • NEWSPAPER • BRADAWL AND SCRAP OF WOOD • PENCIL • A 50 x 3 MM (2 x ⅛ IN) MACHINE SCREW AND THREE NUTS FOR EACH KNOB • PROTECTIVE FACE MASK • FINE SANDPAPER • NON-TOXIC WHITE EMULSION (LATEX) PAINT • PAINTBRUSH • HAIRY STRING • SCISSORS • NON-TOXIC GOLD ACRYLIC PAINT

4 Tear small pieces of tissue paper and dip them into diluted PVA (white) glue. Squeeze and roll them between finger and thumb to make pointed shapes. Press the points firmly into the edges of the discs to attach them. Leave the knobs to dry thoroughly on a wire rack.

6 Screw a machine screw through the middle of each knob and secure it in place with a matching nut. Cover the head of each screw with two layers of papier mâché strips and leave the knobs to dry.

8 Spread a little undiluted PVA (white) glue in the middle of each knob and coil a length of hairy string on to it to make a decorative centre.

5 Cover the knobs with one layer of small papier mâché strips. When they are dry, place each one on a piece of scrap wood and use a bradawl to make a hole in the centre. Widen each hole with a pencil until a machine screw will fit into it.

7 Wearing a protective face mask, lightly sand each knob and prime it with two coats of white emulsion (latex) paint, allowing the first coat to dry thoroughly before the second is added.

9 Paint the tips of the knobs gold. To fix the knobs, mark the centre point of each drawer. Clamp the drawers firmly and drill a hole in the centre. Wind a nut on to the machine-screw shank of each knob. Push the ends of the shanks through the holes in the drawers and add another nut to each. To secure the knobs, tighten all the nuts.

BAY LEAF HERB STAND

THIS DAINTY STAND, INSPIRED BY FRENCH BAKERY SHELVES, IS PERFECT FOR STORING POTS OF FRESH HERBS OR JARS OF SPICES OR DISPLAYING SMALL ORNAMENTS. ITS DELICATE SPIRALS AND PAPIER MACHE BAY LEAVES DISGUISE ITS STRENGTH, WHICH COMES FROM ITS SOLID FRAMEWORK OF HEAVY CORRUGATED CARDBOARD. HERE SPIRALS OF FLORIST'S WIRE DECORATE THE TOPS AND SIDES OF THE SHELVES YET OTHER MOTIFS COULD BE USED, SUCH AS HEARTS OR FLOWERS.

1 Using the templates at the back of the book, measure and mark out all the components, except the border frill, on a sheet of heavy corrugated cardboard. Cut two pieces for the front and sides. Cut a strip of lightweight cardboard, measuring 30 x 2.5 cm (12 x 1 in), and form one long edge into a wavy border. Assemble the stand using PVA (white) glue and masking tape. Cut a thin strip of heavy cardboard and glue it underneath the top shelf to strengthen it. Attach the scalloped trim to the top shelf.

2 Brush diluted PVA (white) glue over all the surfaces of the stand, including underneath. Leave to dry.

3 Tear newspaper into 2.5 cm (1 in) strips. Dip the strips into diluted PVA (white) glue and cover the stand with five layers of papier mâché. Use small, narrow strips to go around the scalloped border on the top shelf. Leave to dry.

4 Trace and cut nine leaf templates from the back of the book on to heavy cardboard. Tear thin strips of newspaper, dipped in diluted PVA (white) glue, and layer each leaf twice. Leave to dry.

5 Using pliers, grasp one end of a length of wire and curl into a spiral, leaving sufficient length to attach to the shelf. Open out the spiral slightly to create a smooth pattern. Repeat to make four matching shelf ends. ▶

MATERIALS AND EQUIPMENT YOU WILL NEED

METAL RULER AND PENCIL • HEAVY AND LIGHTWEIGHT CORRUGATED CARDBOARD • CRAFT KNIFE AND CUTTING MAT •
NON-TOXIC PVA (WHITE) GLUE • MASKING TAPE • PAINTBRUSHES AND PALETTE • NEWSPAPER • TRACING PAPER • ROUND-NOSED PLIERS •
FLORIST'S WIRE • BRADAWL • PROTECTIVE FACE MASK • FINE SANDPAPER • NON-TOXIC EMULSION (LATEX) PAINTS: WHITE AND LIME GREEN •
NON-TOXIC ACRYLIC PAINTS: LIGHT, MEDIUM AND DARK GREEN • NON-TOXIC WATER-BASED ACRYLIC VARNISH

6 Position the wire spirals on the shelves and secure them top and bottom with small pieces of masking tape. Tear narrow strips of newspaper and cover the top (non-spiral) ends only with three layers of papier mâché.

8 Remove the masking tape from the bottom of the wire shelf ends. Wearing a protective face mask, lightly sand the leaves and the stand. Prime them with two coats of white emulsion (latex) paint, allowing each coat to dry thoroughly.

10 Apply light green acrylic paint to the leaves. Add a second, patchy coat of medium green. Paint veins on the front of each leaf, using the darkest green.

7 Use the pliers to cut 8 cm (3¼ in) lengths of florist's wire for the leaf stems. Pierce a hole through the base of each leaf with a bradawl. Dab a little glue on one end of each piece of wire, and push the wires up into the leaves.

9 Paint the stand with two coats of lime green emulsion (latex) paint. When the paint is thoroughly dry, use undiluted PVA (white) glue to fix the free ends of each piece of wire into place on the shelves.

11 Use a bradawl to make a hole for each leaf along the top edge of the stand. Dab a little undiluted PVA (white) glue on to one end of each piece of wire and push into position to form the stem. Seal the stand with a coat of acrylic varnish.

AFRICAN POT

PAPIER MACHE MIMICS THE APPEARANCE OF FIRED CLAY TO STRIKING EFFECT IN THIS AFRICAN-INSPIRED POT. THE BODY OF THE POT IS CONSTRUCTED USING A BALLOON MOULD, AND THE NECK AND FOOT ARE MADE FROM CARDBOARD. THE SURFACE IS COVERED WITH A GENEROUS LAYER OF PAPER PULP, INCISED WITH DELICATE DESIGNS, AND TREATED WITH A THIN WASH OF PAINT THAT SOAKS INTO SOME AREAS, GIVING A DISTRESSED APPEARANCE.

1 Inflate a round balloon and tie the end firmly. Smear a layer of petroleum jelly over the balloon and rest it on a small container. Dip large squares of newspaper into diluted PVA (white) glue and build up four layers of papier mâché, completely covering the balloon. Leave to dry.

2 To make the foot, cut a narrow strip of corrugated cardboard, with the corrugations running crosswise. Then cut a semi-circular strip to form the neck of the pot, and a circle and a long, thin strip of corrugated cardboard to create the lid.

3 Glue and tape the circle and strip together to form the lid. Curve the strip of cardboard that makes the neck, and glue and tape the ends together. Curve the foot and glue and tape this too. Cover all three pieces with strips of brown gummed paper tape to strengthen them. Prick the balloon and invert the pot.

4 Glue and tape the foot in place. Dry, then cover the join with 2–3 layers of papier mâché. Join the neck to the pot and cut an opening in the top of the pot.

▶

MATERIALS AND EQUIPMENT YOU WILL NEED

ROUND BALLOON • PETROLEUM JELLY • SMALL BOWL • NEWSPAPER • NON-TOXIC PVA (WHITE) GLUE • WIDE BRUSH • THIN CORRUGATED CARDBOARD • CRAFT KNIFE AND CUTTING MAT • MASKING TAPE • BROWN GUMMED PAPER TAPE • SCISSORS • PROTECTIVE FACE MASK • THIN RUBBER (LATEX) GLOVES • PAPER PULP (SEE BASIC TECHNIQUES) • MEDIUM- AND FINE-GRADE SANDPAPER • METAL SKEWER • POSTER PAINTS: RAW UMBER AND BURNT SIENNA • HOUSEHOLD SPONGE • PALETTE • PAINTBRUSH • STENCIL CARDBOARD • TWINE • JAPANESE TISSUE PAPER

5 Wearing a face mask and gloves, cover the outside of the pot with a generous layer of paper pulp and allow to dry. Lightly sand the surface, then add a second layer. Cover the outside of the lid in the same way. Leave to dry thoroughly.

7 Mix raw umber and burnt sienna poster paints with water to make thin washes. Dab them on to the pot and lid, using a damp household sponge. Work the paint over the surface to create a patchy, distressed effect.

9 Cut a length of twine that is twice the circumference of the neck of the pot. Fold the twine in half and cover it with thin strips of Japanese tissue paper. Wearing thin rubber (latex) gloves, coat the papered twine with a layer of paper pulp, and allow to dry slightly.

6 Wearing a protective face mask, rub the surface down lightly with medium-grade sandpaper, and finish with fine sandpaper. Use a metal skewer to incise simple patterns, such as rows of lines, in the pulp.

8 Cut simple designs, such as zig-zags and small rectangles, into the stencil cardboard. Place the stencils on the pot and lid, and push paper pulp through the cuts, using a small scrap of corrugated cardboard, to form relief patterns.

10 While the twine is still damp, wrap it around the neck of the pot, pressing it in firmly so that it stays in place when dry.

FOLK ART BOX

THIS ENDEARING LITTLE BOX IS CONSTRUCTED FROM HEAVY CARDBOARD AND PIPE CLEANERS. PAPER PULP IS USED TO MOULD THE HORSE AND BUILD UP AREAS OF LOW RELIEF, AND THE BOX IS PAINTED A DENSE WHITE TO RESEMBLE FIRED CLAY. THE BASE IS COVERED WITH LAYERS OF PAPER. THE DECORATION IS BOLD BUT SPARE, IN BRIGHT PAINTS THAT REINFORCE THE BOX'S FOLK-ART APPEARANCE. HEAVY CORRUGATED CARDBOARD — PERHAPS RECYCLED FROM PACKAGING — ENSURES A STURDY BOX, WHICH WOULD MAKE AN IDEAL PRESENT, ORNAMENT OR TRINKET BOX. THIS BOX IS NOT SUITABLE FOR CHILDREN.

2 To form the lip of the lid, cut a rectangle 13 x 7.5 cm (5¼ x 3 in) from the heavy cardboard and glue to the centre of the underside of the lid.

1 Using a craft knife, cutting mat and metal ruler, cut out two pieces of heavy cardboard, 15 x 10 cm (6 x 4 in) for the lid and base. Cut two pieces of heavy cardboard 15 x 6 cm (6 x 2½ in) for the sides, and two pieces 10 x 6 cm (4 x 2½ in) for the ends of the box. Spread a line of undiluted PVA (white) glue around the inside edge of the box base, and glue and tape the four walls in place.

3 Cut a rectangle of thin cardboard, 8 x 6 cm (3¼ x 2½ in). Place the cardboard on a piece of scrap wood. Using a bradawl, make four holes where the horse's legs will be. For the legs, thread a pipe cleaner through each pair of holes, from the base to the top of the cardboard.

4 To form the horse's body, take a pipe cleaner and thread it around the top of each leg to make a rectangle. Remember to leave an extra loop at the back of the horse for its tail. Use more pipe cleaners to create the neck, head and ears, and to enlarge the main body. ▶

MATERIALS AND EQUIPMENT YOU WILL NEED
CRAFT KNIFE AND CUTTING MAT • PENCIL AND METAL RULER • HEAVY AND LIGHTWEIGHT CORRUGATED CARDBOARD • NON-TOXIC PVA (WHITE) GLUE • MASKING TAPE • BRADAWL AND SCRAP WOOD • PIPE CLEANERS • PAPER PULP (SEE BASIC TECHNIQUES) • PROTECTIVE FACE MASK • THIN RUBBER (LATEX) GLOVES • RECYCLED PAPER • NON-TOXIC PASTE • NON-TOXIC WHITE EMULSION (LATEX) PAINT • PAINTBRUSHES • NON-TOXIC ACRYLIC PAINTS IN A VARIETY OF COLOURS

5 Mix a quantity of paper pulp. Wearing a protective face mask and rubber (latex) gloves, mould the shape of the horse over the pipe-cleaner armature, using pieces of pulp. Leave the horse to dry thoroughly.

7 When the lid is thoroughly dry, tear small squares of recycled paper, coat them with paste glue, and use them to cover the box and lid. Allow them to dry completely.

9 When the emulsion (latex) paint is dry, start to decorate the horse and lid, using acrylic paints.

6 Place the horse and stand in the centre of the lid, and mark the positions of the pipe cleaners that run beneath the stand. Cut two small channels in the lid to accommodate the pipe cleaners, and glue the horse to the lid. Brush a coat of diluted PVA (white) glue over the top of the lid to provide a key, then use small discs of pulp to make a decorative edging around it.

8 Prime the surface of the box and lid with two coats of white emulsion (latex) paint, allowing the first coat to dry thoroughly before the second is added.

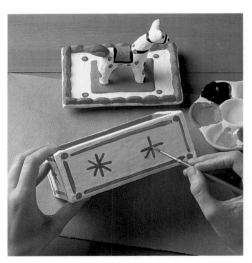

10 Paint the inside of the box and add a simple decoration to each wall.

CHEQUERED DOORS

BATHROOM OR KITCHEN CABINETS ARE OFTEN DULL, BUT YOU CAN TURN THEM INTO STRIKING ITEMS AT MINIMAL COST, USING JUST A FEW LAYERS OF PAPER. TISSUE AND HANDMADE PAPER IN WARM, NEUTRAL COLOURS CONVEY A STYLISH EFFECT, SEALED WITH DILUTED VARNISH TO MAKE THE PAPER HIGHLY PRACTICAL AND CREATE A TRANSLUCENT, INTERESTING TEXTURE. THIS METHOD CAN BE SUITED TO ANY COLOUR SCHEME. GATHER A COLLECTION OF PAPERS THAT MATCH YOUR EXISTING DECOR, AND EXPERIMENT WITH DIFFERENT COLOURS, SHAPES AND DESIGNS. HERE FINELY TEXTURED HANDMADE PAPERS ARE USED.

1 Wearing a protective face mask, lightly sand the front and sides of the door. Apply a coat of acrylic wood primer and leave it to dry thoroughly.

2 Tear pieces of white tissue paper and apply one layer to the front of the door, using diluted PVA (white) glue and a wide brush.

3 Measure the inner recess of the door. With the aid of a metal ruler, tear some squares of yellow ochre and brown handmade paper to fit the space. ▶

MATERIALS AND EQUIPMENT YOU WILL NEED

PROTECTIVE FACE MASK • FINE SANDPAPER • WATER-BASED ACRYLIC WOOD PRIMER • PAINTBRUSHES • WHITE TISSUE PAPER • NON-TOXIC PVA (WHITE) GLUE • WIDE BRUSH • METAL RULER • YELLOW OCHRE AND BROWN HANDMADE PAPER • SHEET OF JAPANESE TISSUE PAPER • THIN CORRUGATED CARDBOARD • SCISSORS • COLOURED TISSUE PAPER • THIN RUBBER (LATEX) GLOVES • MATT OIL VARNISH • WHITE SPIRIT (ALCOHOL)

4 Using diluted PVA (white) glue and a brush, attach the yellow squares to the front of the door in a chequerboard pattern. Tear a rectangle of thin Japanese tissue paper the same size as the inner panel, and glue it over the top of the yellow squares to subdue the colour.

6 Tear irregular-sized strips of coloured tissue paper and glue over the cardboard squares and the sides of the door, using diluted PVA (white) glue and a wide brush.

8 Glue the large brown paper squares between the yellow squares in the door recess. Tear narrow strips of the same paper and glue them around the inside of the recess, covering the edges of the squares. Leave the door to dry thoroughly. Then, wearing thin rubber (latex) gloves, and working in a well-ventilated area, dilute two parts of oil varnish with one part of white spirit (alcohol) and seal the door with two coats.

7 Tear tiny squares of brown and yellow handmade paper and, using diluted PVA (white) glue, stick them on to the centres of the cardboard squares, alternating the colours.

5 Cut small squares from thin cardboard to make a low-relief border, and glue them around the door frame with undiluted PVA (white) glue.

DUCK-EGG BOWL

THE WIDE RANGE OF RECYCLED PAPERS NOW AVAILABLE IN EXCITING COLOURS AND TEXTURES MAKES EXCITING PAPIER MACHE. THIS COOL BLUE BOWL CONSISTS OF LAYERS OF THIN, SPECKLED RECYCLED PAPER. ITS SIMPLE LINES AND UNPAINTED, ROUGH SURFACE GIVE THE BOWL A PLEASINGLY ANTIQUE FEEL. A ROW OF SPIRALS, FORMED FROM PLIABLE FLORIST'S WIRE, DECORATES THE RIM OF THE BOWL CREATING AN ELEGANT FINISH.

1 Spread a thin layer of petroleum jelly inside the mould. Tear the paper into 2.5 cm (1 in) strips. Dip the strips into diluted PVA (white) glue and lay them inside the bowl, overlapping the edges slightly. Apply five layers and leave to dry.

3 Trim the excess paper from around the rim to neaten the edges. If you are not confident of cutting an even curve, draw a pencil line first to guide you.

5 Attach the spirals at equal distances around the inside of the bowl rim, using strips of masking tape. All the spirals should face the same way.

2 Insert a palette knife between the mould and the paper shell and gently separate. When the sides of the paper bowl are free, carefully lever it from the mould. Place the bowl upside down and leave until the underneath is dry.

4 To make the spirals, grasp the end of a length of florist's wire with a pair of round-nosed pliers. Use an even pressure to curl the wire, then open it out slightly with your fingers to form a uniform pattern. Repeat for as many spirals as you need.

6 Cover the masking tape with small pieces of papier mâché to keep the spirals neatly in place. Leave the bowl to dry thoroughly before you use it.

MATERIALS AND EQUIPMENT YOU WILL NEED

PETROLEUM JELLY • OLD BOWL TO USE AS MOULD • THIN SPECKLED RECYCLED PAPER • DILUTED NON-TOXIC PVA (WHITE) GLUE •
FLEXIBLE PALETTE KNIFE • SCISSORS • PENCIL (OPTIONAL) • FLORIST'S WIRE • ROUND-NOSED PLIERS • MASKING TAPE

COLLECTOR'S SHOWCASE

IT CAN BE TRICKY TO DISPLAY COLLECTIONS OF SMALL OBJECTS WITHOUT CREATING CLUTTER. THIS PAPIER MACHE SHOWCASE FITS THE BILL PERFECTLY, MAKING A STYLISH HOME FOR A GROUP OF MINIATURE ITEMS. THE THEME OF THE COLLECTION CLEVERLY COMPLEMENTS THE RESTRAINED, SUBTLE COLOURS OF THE DISPLAY CASE. THE CASE IS CONSTRUCTED FROM MOUNTING BOARD FOR SOLIDITY, AND EMBELLISHED WITH A PAPIER MACHE FINISH.

1 Decide on the dimensions of your display case. For the back, cut two identical pieces from a sheet of mounting board. Make a small central slit 4 cm (1½ in) down from the top of one piece. Push the shanks of a split ring (wire) hanger through the slit, open them out, and keep them in place with glue and masking tape. Glue the pieces of board together, with the shanks of the hanger to the inside.

2 Measure out another piece of board the same size. Add an arch at the top and cut out the entire shape. Use this as a template to cut another piece and glue the two pieces together. Mark out the windows on the front.

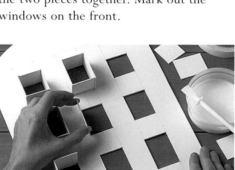

3 Place the case front on a cutting mat and carefully cut out each window. Measure the depth of your largest object, and cut strips of board as wide as this, to fit around each window. Glue and tape the strips in place.

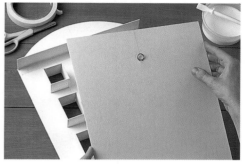

4 Cut four strips of board 4 cm (1½ in) wide to fit along the top and bottom of the case front on the inside. Glue them together and glue and tape them in place. Glue around the window frames, and glue and tape the back and front together.

5 Cut four strips of board for the sides. Glue them together and glue and tape them in place. Cut two narrow strips of board and glue them together to make a ledge for the front of the case. Glue the ledge centrally, below the windows. ▶

MATERIALS AND EQUIPMENT YOU WILL NEED

TWO SHEETS MOUNTING BOARD • CRAFT KNIFE AND CUTTING MAT • METAL RULER AND PENCIL • BRASS SPLIT RING (WIRE) HANGER • NON-TOXIC PVA (WHITE) GLUE • MASKING TAPE • NEWSPAPER • CARDBOARD • NON-TOXIC WHITE EMULSION (LATEX) PAINT • PAINTBRUSHES • GOUACHE PAINTS: BROWN, LIGHT GREY AND SILVER • PROTECTIVE FACE MASK • FINE SANDPAPER • BEADING WIRE AND PAIR OF PLIERS • WHITE CHINA BEADS • DUTCH METAL LEAF • ORNAMENTAL BUTTON

6 Cover the entire display case with two layers of papier mâché squares, pasted smoothly over the surface. Make sure that the papier mâché is pushed neatly into the corners of the windows. Support each window frame with strips of cardboard.

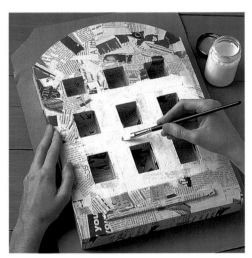

7 Prime the display case with a coat of white emulsion (latex) paint and allow it to dry thoroughly.

8 Apply a coat of the brown paint to the display case. Leave to dry. Mix the grey and brown gouache with the white emulsion (latex) paint and re-paint the case. Paint the inside of the central window silver. Cover the surface with a thin coat of white emulsion (latex) paint, and wearing a protective face mask, lightly rub it down to reveal the colours beneath.

9 To make supports for the decorative row of beads, cut a short length of fine beading wire for each bead. Thread the bead on to the middle of its wire, and twist the ends of the wire together with small pliers to make "stalks".

10 Paint an outline around the central window and a small square at the top. Apply metal leaf around the central window and glue the button to the centre of the square. Use undiluted PVA (white) glue to fix each object into its window. Stand the display case upright, and leave the glue to dry thoroughly.

11 Divide the ledge into six equal sections. Using a craft knife and metal ruler, cut a shallow notch at each mark. Spread a little undiluted PVA (white) glue into each notch and press the wire stalks of the beads into them. Leave the case to dry thoroughly.

SCROLLED WALL BRACKET

THIS IMPRESSIVE WALL BRACKET, WITH ITS ECHOES OF IONIC COLUMNS, IS FINISHED WITH A LAYER OF CHINESE NEWSPAPER AND LEFT UNPAINTED FOR AN ELEGANT, MINIMALIST LOOK. IT COULD BE PAINTED IN GOLD OR SILVER FOR AN EXTRA AIR OF CLASSICAL SPLENDOUR, OR BE MATCHED TO AN EXISTING COLOUR SCHEME. THE ARMATURE OF CORRUGATED CARDBOARD AND WIRE MESH CAN BE MADE INTO ORNATE SHAPES. IT IS FIRST ENCASED IN A LAYER OF TISSUE PAPER STRIPS, WHICH CONTRACT AS THEY DRY, PULLING THE ARMATURE INTO A TAUT SHAPE THAT IS EASY TO COVER. THE BRACKET IS NOT SUITABLE FOR HEAVY OBJECTS.

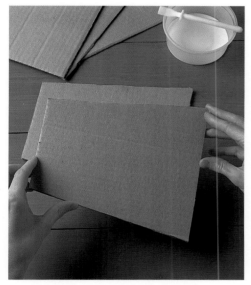

1 To make the bracket, draw out three rectangles of cardboard measuring 20 x 16 cm (8 x 6¼ in). Draw another three wedge-shaped pieces, measuring 20 cm (8 in) long, and 18 cm (7 in) tapering to 12 cm (4¾ in) wide. Cut out all the pieces, using a craft knife and cutting mat. Glue the three pieces of each size together, using undiluted PVA (white) glue.

2 To assemble the bracket, place the rectangle and wedge-shaped pieces of cardboard at right angles and using undiluted PVA (white) glue, stick and tape them together.

3 Wearing protective leather gloves, cut a rectangle of wire mesh measuring 60 x 23 cm (24 x 9 in). Snip off any spurs of wire and dispose of them safely. Turn over the long edges of the mesh by 5 cm (2 in) at the top and 2 cm (¾ in) at the bottom, so that the resulting shape is slightly tapered. ▶

MATERIALS AND EQUIPMENT YOU WILL NEED

METAL RULER AND PENCIL • HEAVY CORRUGATED CARDBOARD • CRAFT KNIFE AND CUTTING MAT • NON-TOXIC PVA (WHITE) GLUE • MASKING TAPE • PROTECTIVE LEATHER GLOVES • SCISSORS • 6 x 6 MM (¼ x ¼ IN) WIRE MESH • WIRE CUTTERS • NEWSPAPER • TISSUE PAPER • NON-TOXIC PASTE • THICK CORD • CHINESE NEWSPAPER • METAL EYELETS • STRONG, CLEAR GLUE

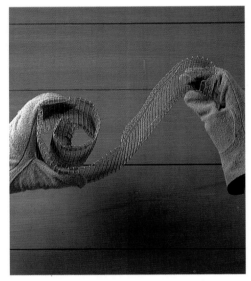

4 Starting at the widest end of the mesh shape, gently roll it into a scroll. Roll the narrower end in the opposite direction to form a second, smaller scroll. The scrolled mesh should sit neatly inside the bracket.

6 Tear wide strips of tissue paper and coat them very lightly with paste glue. Cover the whole scroll with one layer of tissue paper strips, paying special attention to the sides, so that the scroll is a solid shape. Leave the bracket to dry thoroughly.

8 Draw wavy lines down either side of the front of the scroll and a straight line down the centre. Glue lengths of thick cord along the lines to create a low-relief design.

5 Place the scroll inside the bracket and tape it into position. Twist a sheet of newspaper and stuff it inside the larger scroll to pad out the space.

7 Apply three layers of newspaper strips over the whole of the bracket. Run the papier mâché strips from the wire mesh to the cardboard to fill in the gaps. Leave to dry completely.

9 Using squares of Chinese newspaper, cover the entire bracket again. Make sure that the paper is neatly applied, as this is the final layer. Screw two eyelets into the back of the bracket and secure them in place with a dab of strong glue.

EXOTIC BLIND PULLS

THESE GORGEOUS BLIND PULLS, INSPIRED BY THE COSTUMES AND COLOURS OF THE EAST, CAN BE ADAPTED TO AN INFINITE VARIETY OF DESIGNS. THEY ARE MOULDED ON CARDBOARD ARMATURES, USING SMALL PELLETS OF PAPER PULP, THEN COVERED WITH PAPIER MACHE STRIPS TO GIVE A SMOOTH SURFACE. THE STRIPS ARE TORN FROM UNPRINTED NEWSPAPER, KNOWN AS NEWSPRINT. IF NEWSPRINT IS NOT AVAILABLE, ORDINARY NEWSPAPER WILL WORK JUST AS WELL.

1 Trace the teardrop shape from the template at the back of the book, and transfer it twice to thin white card. Cut out both pieces.

2 Cut a length of string to fit from top to bottom of the teardrop with a generous overlap, and keep it loosely in the centre of the cardboard shape with two small strips of masking tape.

3 Wearing a face mask and gloves, use pellets of paper pulp to build up the curved shape of each half of the pull. Keep the same depth of pulp on both pieces of cardboard, and mould it so that the sides of the teardrop taper gently. Leave both halves to dry on a wire cake rack.

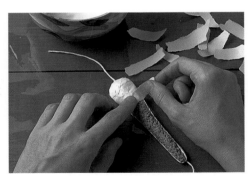

4 Glue the halves together, back to back. Tear small strips of newsprint and dip in diluted PVA (white) glue. Cover the pull with one or two layers of papier mâché strips and leave to dry.

5 Decorate using the acrylic paints. (If using newspaper, first prime with two coats of the emulsion (latex) paint.)

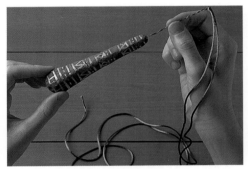

6 Remove the string from the centre of the teardrop. Cut the satin cord to the required length. Bend a piece of wire in half to make a needle, place the cord in the loop, and twist the ends of the wire together. Thread the cord through the teardrop and remove the wire. Add small beads above and below the teardrop to secure the cord. Varnish twice to seal.

MATERIALS AND EQUIPMENT YOU WILL NEED

TRACING PAPER AND PENCIL • THIN WHITE CARDBOARD • SCISSORS • STRING • MASKING TAPE • PROTECTIVE FACE MASK • THIN RUBBER (LATEX) GLOVES • PAPER PULP (SEE BASIC TECHNIQUES) • OLD WIRE CAKE RACK • NON-TOXIC PVA (WHITE) GLUE • NEWSPRINT OR NEWSPAPER • NON-TOXIC WHITE EMULSION (LATEX) PAINT • NON-TOXIC ACRYLIC PAINTS IN A VARIETY OF COLOURS • PAINTBRUSHES • SATIN CORD • THIN FLORIST'S WIRE • SMALL BEADS • NON-TOXIC, WATER-BASED ACRYLIC VARNISH

CINDERELLA CHAIR

AN EVERYDAY KITCHEN CHAIR BLOSSOMS INTO A ROCOCO PROFUSION OF CURLICUES AND FLAMBOYANT FRILLS — ALL DEVISED FROM CORRUGATED CARDBOARD. WHEN THE MAKEOVER IS COMPLETE, THE CHAIR IS COATED WITH A GENEROUS LAYER OF PAPER PULP THAT HARDENS AND STRENGTHENS THE DETAILS.

THE CARDBOARD IS ATTACHED WITH CONTACT ADHESIVE, WHICH IS VERY STRONG SMELLING AND SHOULD BE USED IN THE OPEN AIR IF POSSIBLE. IF NOT, WORK IN A WELL-VENTILATED SPACE, AND TAKE FREQUENT BREAKS. ALWAYS WEAR THIN RUBBER (LATEX) GLOVES AND A RESPIRATORY MASK WHEN USING THE ADHESIVE.

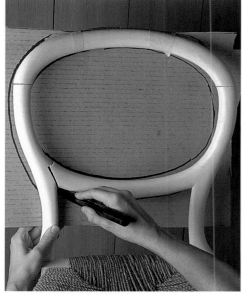

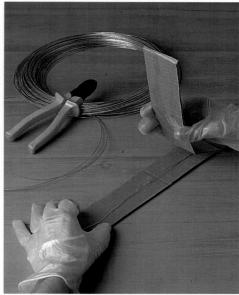

1 Tape a sheet of thin corrugated cardboard to the back of the chair and draw around the outline of the frame, using a marker pen. Remove the cardboard and cut out the shape. Wearing a protective face mask and rubber (latex) gloves whilst using the contact adhesive, glue the cardboard to the front of the chair.

2 Cut long thin strips of cardboard with the corrugations running vertically across. Glue the strips around the sides and front of the chair seat. Cut a cover from corrugated cardboard to fit the top of the chair, and glue it in place.

3 Cut two identical strips of 6 cm (2½ in) wide corrugated cardboard, to run around the edge from the chair seat to the centre top of the chair. Cut a piece of thin galvanized wire the same length as the strips, and sandwich it centrally between the two. Glue the strips together. Repeat to make another strip. ▶

MATERIALS AND EQUIPMENT YOU WILL NEED

THIN CORRUGATED CARDBOARD WITH EXPOSED CORRUGATIONS • MASKING TAPE • MARKER PEN • SCISSORS • PROTECTIVE FACE MASK • THIN RUBBER (LATEX) GLOVES • CONTACT ADHESIVE • THIN GALVANIZED WIRE • WIRE CUTTERS • WIDE PAINTBRUSH • PAPER PULP (SEE BASIC TECHNIQUES)

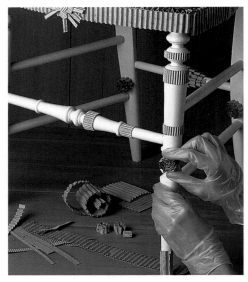

4 Curve a wired strip of cardboard around one half of the chair-back outline. Roll the top and bottom of the strip into wide curls and glue it in place. Cut a very long, narrow ribbon of cardboard and use it to cover the edges of the strip. Repeat to make the curlicues for the other half of the chair.

6 Cut strips of cardboard to cover the lower portions of the chair back, just above the seat. Cut more narrow strips and glue them to the top edge of the seat.

8 Cut strips of cardboard and glue them around the legs and struts of the chair. Form cardboard rosettes and glue them to the front of the chair legs. Make swirls of cardboard for the lower edge of the seat and the front of the legs.

7 Cut spirals, small flowers, bows and other decorations from cardboard, and glue them to the chair back and around the seat as embellishment.

9 Using a wide brush, and wearing rubber (latex) gloves and face mask, apply a generous coat of paper pulp all over the surface of the chair. Allow it to dry thoroughly, to strengthen the cardboard.

5 Cut a 3 cm (1¼ in) wide strip of cardboard and glue it around the inside edge of the seat back to cover the raw edges of the cardboard cover.

SCALLOPED FRUIT DISH

THIS ELEGANT PEDESTAL DISH IS A CONTEMPORARY INTERPRETATION OF THE PRESSED GLASS AND MOULDED FRUIT PLATES THAT HAVE ADORNED MANY A COUNTRY SIDEBOARD. GRACEFUL AND UNDERSTATED, ITS HARMONIOUS SHAPE AND SMOOTH WHITE SURFACE WILL COMPLEMENT ITS COLOURFUL CONTENTS. THE PLATE'S ARMATURE IS CONSTRUCTED FROM FINE WIRE MESH, MANIPULATED TO MAKE A FLUTED EDGE. THE STAND IS MADE SEPARATELY FROM CORRUGATED CARDBOARD, AND BUILT UP USING PAPER PULP TO GIVE A CARVED APPEARANCE. SEVERAL LAYERS OF PAPIER MACHE ENSURE AN EVEN SURFACE.

1 Draw a circle with a diameter of 30 cm (12 in) on a sheet of paper and cut it out to make a template for the dish. Tape the template to a piece of wire mesh. Wearing protective leather gloves, carefully cut around the template, using wire cutters. Trim away any sharp spurs of wire around the circle and dispose of them safely.

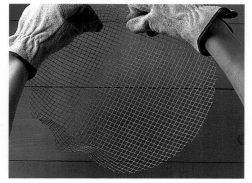

2 Pull and push the rim of the mesh disc into a fluted shape. Make sure that the fluted curves are regular, and that the base of the plate remains flat.

3 Tear wide strips of tissue paper and layer them over both sides of the plate, using paste glue. Use thinner strips of paper to cover the rim. Leave to dry.

4 To make the stand, draw a circle with a diameter of 10 cm (4 in) on a sheet of paper and cut it out to make a template. Cut out four circles from thin cardboard. Draw and cut a wavy edge around two of the circles. Cut a strip of thin cardboard measuring 18 x 5 cm (7 x 2 in). Make sure that the corrugations run from top to bottom of the stand so that you can roll it easily. ▶

MATERIALS AND EQUIPMENT YOU WILL NEED

THIN PAPER • PAIR OF COMPASSES AND PENCIL • SCISSORS • MASKING TAPE • PIECE OF 6 x 6 MM (¼ x ¼ IN) WIRE MESH •
PROTECTIVE LEATHER GLOVES • WIRE CUTTERS • TISSUE PAPER • NON-TOXIC PASTE • TRACING PAPER • THIN CORRUGATED CARDBOARD •
NON-TOXIC PVA (WHITE) GLUE • THIN RUBBER (LATEX) GLOVES • PROTECTIVE FACE MASK • PAPER PULP (SEE BASIC TECHNIQUES) • NEWSPAPER •
NON-TOXIC WHITE EMULSION (LATEX) PAINT • PAINTBRUSH • WATER-BASED ACRYLIC VARNISH (OPTIONAL)

5 Glue two of the circles together, using undiluted PVA (white) glue, then glue the two flower shapes on top. Roll the strip of cardboard tightly, and secure the end with a piece of masking tape. Glue and tape the roll in the centre of the flower shapes. Wearing gloves and a face mask, mix a small quantity of paper pulp and use it to build up and shape the base, following the outline of the flower.

7 Tear squares of newspaper and coat them with the paste glue. Cover the entire plate with six to eight layers of papier mâché squares, then leave it to dry thoroughly.

6 Glue the two remaining cardboard circles together. When the pulp covering the base is completely dry, glue and tape the base to the middle of them. Attach the finished stand to the centre of the underside of the plate.

8 When the plate is dry, apply two coats of white emulsion (latex) paint, allowing the first coat to dry completely before the second is added. Seal the fruit dish with two coats of matt acrylic varnish, if desired.

HERALDIC WALL VASE

THIS SMALL WALL VASE HAS A HERALDIC LOOK, DERIVED FROM ITS SHIELD-LIKE SHAPE AND METALLIC FINISH, HIGHLIGHTED BY TOUCHES OF BRONZE. THE AGED METAL APPEARANCE IS ACHIEVED BY APPLYING SEVERAL COATS OF GOUACHE PAINT MIXED WITH WHITE EMULSION (LATEX) PAINT, THEN LIGHTLY RUBBING DOWN THE SURFACE TO REVEAL PATCHES OF THE DIFFERENT LAYERS OF COLOUR. THE VASE HOLDS A CLEAN MEDICINE BOTTLE WITH THICK GLASS WALLS, TO DISPLAY DRIED OR FRESH FLOWERS. MEASURE YOUR INNER CONTAINER CAREFULLY TO ENSURE ENOUGH ROOM FOR EASY REMOVAL.

1 Trace the vase shapes from the template at the back of the book, and transfer one back and two fronts to a sheet of mounting cardboard. Place the cardboard on a cutting mat, and cut out one front and one back. Glue them together using undiluted PVA (white) glue, then carefully cut out the hole at the top of the vase back designed for hanging.

2 Measure the height and width of the bottle. Draw a central rectangle on the vase back that is 0.5 cm (¼ in) larger all round than the bottle. Place the bottle inside the rectangle and measure its depth. Cut three strips of cardboard 0.5 cm (¼ in) wider than the depth of the bottle to fit around the sides and base of the rectangle, and glue and tape them in place. Cut another rectangle of cardboard to cover the front of the bottle and glue and tape it into position, so that the bottle is boxed in.

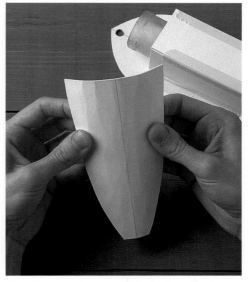

3 Cut out the second vase front and draw a central line down it. Using your fingers, carefully bend the front into a shallow curve from the central line outwards. Place the curved front centrally over the vase, resting it against the front wall of the box that contains the bottle. Glue and tape it firmly in place to strengthen the joints. ▶

MATERIALS AND EQUIPMENT YOU WILL NEED

TRACING PAPER AND PENCIL • SHEET OF MOUNTING CARDBOARD • MASKING TAPE • CRAFT KNIFE AND CUTTING MAT • NON-TOXIC PVA (WHITE) GLUE • METAL RULER • SMALL GLASS BOTTLE • SCISSORS • THIN, FLEXIBLE CARDBOARD • NEWSPAPER • NON-TOXIC POWDERED GLUE PASTE • NON-TOXIC WHITE EMULSION (LATEX) PAINT • PAINTBRUSHES • GOUACHE PAINTS: BLUE, GREY, BROWN, BRONZE AND SILVER • PROTECTIVE FACE MASK • FINE SANDPAPER • WATER-BASED GOLD SIZE • BRONZE DUTCH METAL LEAF • SOFT BRUSH • ORNAMENTAL BUTTON

4 To make the top of the vase front, hold scraps of cardboard over the openings around the shoulders of the bottle and draw round the shapes. Cut out the two resulting pieces, and glue and tape them in place. Stand the vase on a scrap of card and draw around it to make the base. Cut it out and glue and tape it in position.

5 Place the vase on a strip of thin, flexible cardboard and draw around the outline to make one side piece. Draw around the other side, then cut out both pieces and glue and tape them in place.

6 Using glue paste, cover the vase with two layers of papier mâché squares. Leave the vase to dry thoroughly in between applying layers. Press the paper right into the areas around the joins to give them extra strength. Leave to dry.

7 Prime the surface inside and out with a coat of white emulsion (latex) paint and allow to dry.

8 Make two tones of bluish grey paint and one of warm brown by mixing gouache with white emulsion (latex) paint. Apply to the vase, allowing each coat to dry thoroughly before the next is added. When the final coat is dry, and wearing a protective face mask, lightly rub down the surface of the vase to reveal patches of the different coloured layers.

9 Paint the outlines of a small square near the top of the vase front. Apply a thin coat of water-based gold size to the square and leave it to become tacky (about 20 minutes). Apply a scrap of bronze metal leaf to the sized area with a soft brush, then glue an ornamental button in the square. Add decorative details to the sides of the vase, using bronze and silver gouache paints.

PETAL PICTURE FRAME

P LUMP, LUSTROUS PETALS GIVE THIS CAMEO FRAME A SUNNY AIR. ITS FLUTED EDGES ARE BUILT UP FROM PAPER PULP ON A CARDBOARD ARMATURE, WHICH DRIES TO A FIRM CONSISTENCY. THIS METHOD IS SUITABLE FOR MAKING AN ARRAY OF DIFFERENTLY SHAPED FRAMES WHICH ARE IDEAL FOR DISPLAYING CAMEO-SIZED PICTURES. THE FINISH IS A COAT OF GILT CREAM THAT RESEMBLES SILVER LEAF, BUT IS MUCH EASIER TO APPLY. SUSPENDED FROM WIDE, GROSGRAIN RIBBON, THE FRAME TAKES ON THE APPEARANCE OF A MEDALLION; VARY THE CHOICE OF RIBBON TO MATCH YOUR COLOUR SCHEME.

1 Trace and transfer the frame template at the back of the book to a piece of thin cardboard or paper and cut it out to make a template. Draw around the template on to a piece of heavy corrugated cardboard. Place on a cutting mat and cut out the frame, using a craft knife.

2 Cut a short length of thin copper wire and bend it over to make a loop. Push the ends of the wire into the top of one of the petals to make a hanger for the frame. Secure the hanger in place with undiluted PVA (white) glue.

3 Spread diluted PVA (white) glue over the front of the frame then, wearing rubber (latex) gloves and a face mask, build up the fluted surface with paper pulp. Use a modelling tool to help you to mould the pulp. ▶

MATERIALS AND EQUIPMENT YOU WILL NEED

TRACING PAPER AND PENCIL • THIN CARDBOARD OR PAPER • SCISSORS • HEAVY CORRUGATED CARDBOARD • CRAFT KNIFE AND CUTTING MAT • THIN COPPER WIRE AND WIRE CUTTERS • NON-TOXIC PVA (WHITE) GLUE • THIN RUBBER (LATEX) GLOVES • PROTECTIVE FACE MASK • PAPER PULP (SEE BASIC TECHNIQUES) • MODELLING TOOL • OLD WIRE CAKE RACK • RECYCLED PAPER • NON-TOXIC PASTE • PAINTBRUSHES • NON-TOXIC ACRYLIC GESSO • NON-TOXIC STEEL BLUE ACRYLIC PAINT • SILVER GILT CREAM • SOFT POLISHING CLOTH

4 Mould a ring around the opening of the frame, using small pellets of paper pulp. Leave to dry thoroughly on an old wire cake rack.

6 Prime the surface of the frame with two coats of acrylic gesso. Allow to dry, then add a coat of steel blue acrylic paint.

7 When the paint is dry, apply a coat of silver gilt cream to the frame, following the manufacturer's instructions.

5 When the frame is dry, tear small, thin strips of recycled paper and coat them with paste glue. Cover the entire frame with three layers of strips and leave it to dry thoroughly.

8 Gently polish the surface of the frame, using a soft cloth, to add depth and lustre to the silver finish.

FRAGRANT POMANDERS

ONCE BELIEVED TO PROTECT THE WEARER AGAINST INFECTION AND DISEASE, SWEET-SMELLING POMANDERS HAVE BEEN POPULAR FOR CENTURIES. ORIGINALLY BALLS OF AROMATIC HERBS, CARRIED AROUND TO COUNTER GERMS AND NASTY SMELLS, THEY EVOLVED INTO ROUND, PERFORATED CONTAINERS INTO WHICH THE HERBS WERE PLACED. THESE DELICATELY COLOURED PAPIER MACHE POMANDERS ARE MADE USING RUBBER BALLS AS MOULDS, AND FILLED WITH DRIED LAVENDER TO PERFUME A ROOM, OR DRAWERS AND WARDROBES, WITH A LOVELY LINGERING FRAGRANCE.

1 Smear a thin layer of petroleum jelly over the surface of each rubber ball so that it will be easy to remove the papier mâché when it is dry.

2 Tear small, narrow strips of newspaper and coat them with the glue paste. Cover each ball with six layers of strips, and stand each in an old egg cup to dry.

3 When the papier mâché is dry, draw a line around each ball to divide it into two equal halves. Secure each ball on a cutting mat with a blob of re-usable putty adhesive and cut carefully around the line, repositioning the ball as necessary. Gently separate the paper shells and leave them face-up to dry.

4 When the shells are dry, glue them back together with PVA (white) glue, aligning the cut edges precisely. Cover the joins with two layers of small, thin papier mâché strips and leave them to dry.

5 Place each dry pomander on a piece of scrap wood and pierce holes in the top with the bradawl. Cut a thin section of cork into quarters. Make a small hole for the cork in the bottom of each pomander.

6 Prime the pomanders with a coat of white emulsion (latex) paint, then a coat of coloured paint, avoiding the holes. Using a paper funnel, fill each pomander with lavender and seal with the cork. Tie a ribbon bow around each pomander. Keep the ribbons in place with a blob of PVA (white) glue and pearl-headed pins.

MATERIALS AND EQUIPMENT YOU WILL NEED

PETROLEUM JELLY • SMALL SOLID RUBBER BALLS • NEWSPAPER • NON-TOXIC POWDERED GLUE PASTE • EGG CUPS • PENCIL • RE-USABLE PUTTY ADHESIVE • CRAFT KNIFE AND CUTTING MAT • NON-TOXIC PVA (WHITE) GLUE • SCRAP WOOD • BRADAWL • ROUND CORK • NON-TOXIC EMULSION (LATEX) PAINTS: WHITE AND A VARIETY OF COLOURS • PAINTBRUSHES • DRIED LAVENDER • DECORATIVE RIBBON • PEARL-HEADED PINS

STAFFORDSHIRE DOGS

THIS HANDSOME PAIR OF SPANIELS IS BASED ON THOSE MADE AT THE STAFFORDSHIRE POTTERIES IN ENGLAND DURING THE 19TH CENTURY. ONCE A COMMON SIGHT IN PARLOURS, SITTING AT EITHER END OF THE MANTELPIECE, STAFFORDSHIRE DOGS CAME IN SEVERAL BREEDS, INCLUDING POODLES, BUT THE MOST POPULAR WERE THE SPANIELS, WITH THEIR MOURNFUL EYES. THESE DOGS ARE MADE FROM PULPED TISSUE PAPER OVER A CHICKEN-WIRE ARMATURE, AND THEIR FEATURES ARE MODELLED FROM MORE SMALL PELLETS OF TISSUE PAPER. REMEMBER TO CUT AND HANDLE THE CHICKEN WIRE WITH CARE.

1 Wearing leather gloves and using wire cutters, cut a body and two stand pieces for each dog, as shown. Trim the edges of the chicken wire, if necessary, to remove sharp spurs, and dispose of the clippings safely.

3 Push the tops of the stands into position, inserting them from underneath. Make sure that no sharp edges are protruding, then use thin wire to bind the two pieces together. Place each dog on its stand, and attach it with thin wire.

5 Make more tissue paper pulp, and use small pellets to build up the dogs' features, such as ears, muzzle and legs. Leave the dogs to dry thoroughly.

2 Gently bend the edges of the dogs' bodies to shape them, remembering to make a left- and a right-facing dog. Lace the ends of each stand side piece together using thin florist's wire.

4 Dip soft tissue paper into diluted PVA (white) glue and squeeze it out to form a ball of pulp. Cover the armatures with a layer of pulp, and leave the dogs to dry overnight.

6 Prime the surface of the dogs with two coats of white emulsion (latex) paint. Using black acrylic paint, apply the dogs' facial features and markings. Add a small collar and chain. When the paint is dry, seal the surface of the dogs with a coat of matt acrylic varnish.

MATERIALS AND EQUIPMENT YOU WILL NEED

FINE-GAUGE CHICKEN WIRE • PROTECTIVE LEATHER GLOVES • WIRE CUTTERS • THIN FLORIST'S WIRE • SOFT TISSUE PAPER • NON-TOXIC DILUTED PVA (WHITE) GLUE • NON-TOXIC WHITE EMULSION (LATEX) PAINT • PAINTBRUSHES • BLACK ACRYLIC PAINT • MATT ACRYLIC VARNISH

TEMPLATES

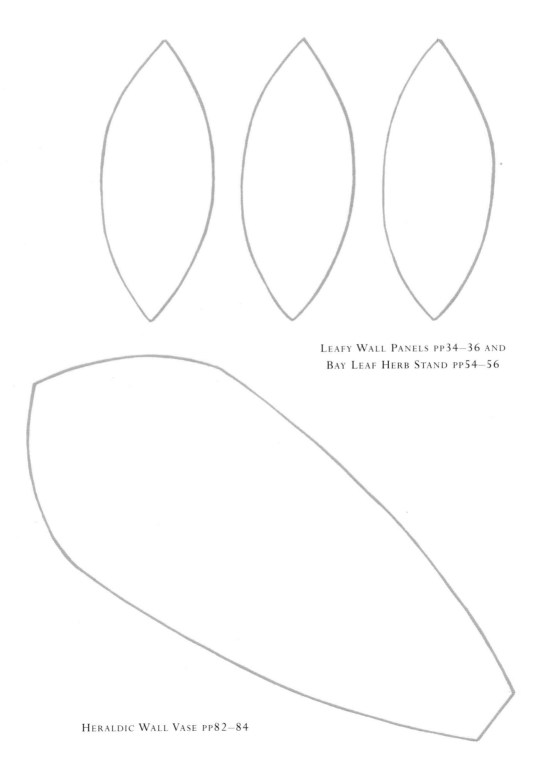

LEAFY WALL PANELS PP34–36 AND
BAY LEAF HERB STAND PP54–56

HERALDIC WALL VASE PP82–84

GILDED FINIALS PP42–44

PETAL PICTURE FRAME PP85–87

EXOTIC BLIND PULLS PP74–75

BAY LEAF HERB STAND pp54–56

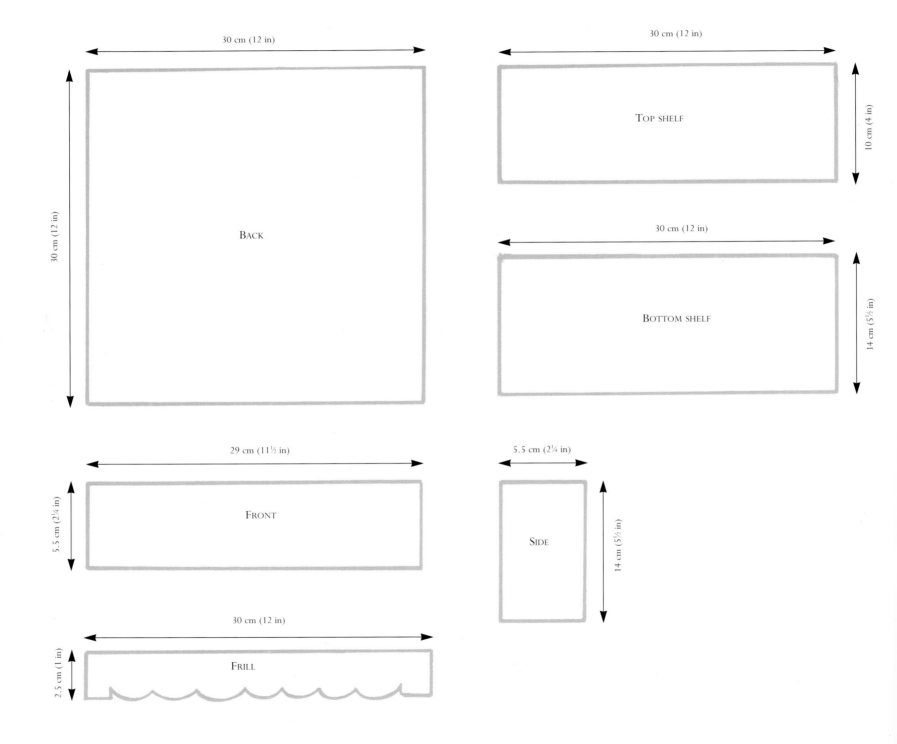

30 cm (12 in)

BACK

30 cm (12 in)

30 cm (12 in)

TOP SHELF

10 cm (4 in)

30 cm (12 in)

BOTTOM SHELF

14 cm (5½ in)

29 cm (11½ in)

FRONT

5.5 cm (2¼ in)

5.5 cm (2¼ in)

SIDE

14 cm (5½ in)

30 cm (12 in)

FRILL

2.5 cm (1 in)

ACKNOWLEDGEMENTS

The author and publishers would like
to thank the following artists for the
projects and gallery pieces
photographed in this book:

Julie Arkell p14
Claire Attridge p13, 14, 15
Lisa Brown p74–75
Hannah Downes p13, 15
Neil Hadfield p90–91
Emma Hardy p32–33, 71–73, 79–81,
88–89
Deborah Schneebeli Morrell p26–28,
60–62, 85–87
Kerry Skinner p45–47, 57–59, 63–65,
76–78
Caroline Waite p12, 13, 14, 15, 37–39,
68–70, 82–84

SUPPLIERS

The publishers would like to thank the
following for supplying the props for
photography:

Joss Graham Oriental Textiles
10 Eccleston Street
London SW1 9LT

V V Rouleaux
10 Symons Street
London SW3 2TJ

David and Charles Wainwright
63 Portobello Road
London W11 3DB

The Old Station
72 Loampit Hill
London SE13

PICTURE CREDITS
The publishers would like to thank the
following agencies for permission to
reproduce pictures in this book:

p8, Christie's Images/Bridgeman Art
Library London (top), Victoria and
Albert Museum (bottom); p9, Victoria
and Albert Museum/Bridgeman Art
Library London (top), Private
Collection/Bridgeman Art Library
London (bottom); p10, Bonhams,
London/Bridgeman Art Library
London (top), Private Collection/
Bridgeman Art Library London
(bottom); p11, David Lavender
(top and bottom).

SOURCES
Boger, Ade Louise, and Boger,
Batterson H., *Dictionary of Antiques and
the Decorative Arts*: Charles Scribner and
Sons, 1957.

Ceilings, Carton Pierre, *Papier-mâché
and Patent Fibrous Plaster Works*: George
Jackson and Sons, 1885.

Fleming John, and Honour, Hugh,
Penguin Dictionary of Decorative Arts:
Penguin, 1977.

Gloag, John, *Short Dictionary of
Furniture*: George Allen and Unwin,
1969.

Jarvis, Simon, *19th Century Papier
Mâché*: HMSO, 1973.

Masuoka, Susan N., En Calavera: *The
Papier-mâché Art of the Linares Family*:
UCLA Fowler Museum, 1994.

Osborne, Harold (ed.), *Oxford
Companion to the Decorative Arts*:
OUP, 1975.

Rush, Peter, *Papier Mâché*: Canongate
Publishing, 1980.

INDEX